RESPONDING TO THE WORD

RESPONDING TO THE WORD

A Biblical Spirituality

JEROME KODELL, O.S.B.

ALBA · HOUSE   NEW · YORK

SOCIETY OF ST. PAUL, 2187 VICTORY BLVD., STATEN ISLAND, NEW YORK 10314

Grateful acknowledgment is made to the following publishers for the reuse of material written by Jerome Kodell: "The Biblical Word," *The Bible Today,* October 1971, pp. 440-446. *"Lectio Divina* and the Sacramental Power of the Word of God." *Benedictines,* Fall-Winter 1975, pp. 76-87. "Living with and Unpredictabl God," *Sisters Today,* April 1975, pp. 441-449.

Scripture texts used are taken from the *New American Bible,* copyright c 1970, by the Confraternity of Christian Doctrine, Washington, D. C., used by permission of copyright owner. All rights reserved.

Library of Congress Cataloging in Publication Data

Kodell, Jerome.
    Responding to the Word.

    Includes bibliographies.
    1. Spiritual life--Catholic authors. I. Title.
BX2350.2.K587   248'.48'2   77-20252
ISBN 0-8189-0360-0

Nihil Obstat:
Richard T. Adams, M.A.
Censor Librorum

Imprimatur:
✝ *James P. Mahoney, D.D.*
Vicar General, Archdiocese of New York
October 13, 1977

Produced in the United States of
America by the Fathers and Brothers of the
Society of St. Paul, 2187 Victory Boulevard,
Staten Island, New York, 10314, as part of their
communications apostolate.

1 2 3 4 5 6 7 8 9 (Current Printing: first digit).

DEDICATION

To Father Michael Lensing, O.S.B.

VATICAN II DOCUMENTS

Ad Gentes, Decree on the Church's Missionary Activity
Dei Verbum, Dogmatic Constitution on Divine Revelation
Gaudium et Spes, Pastoral Constitution on the Church in
    the Modern World
Lumen Gentium, Dogmatic Constitution on the Church
Presbyterorum Ordinis, Decree on the Ministry and Life
    of Priests
Sacrosanctum Concilium, Constitution on the Sacred
    Liturgy
Unitatis Redintegratio, Decree on Ecumenism

CONTENTS

INTRODUCTION

Spirituality is a glamorous word. It brings to mind the great saints of our Christian past, desert monks in their coarse garments, mystics in their transports of prayer. It means library shelves loaded with books on asceticism and contemplation. So it is also a frightening word. Who is worthy to sit in such company, to scale such scholarly heights? But spirituality is really very ordinary. Each of us has a spirituality whether we are aware of it or not. A person's spirituality is simply his relationship to God. This is something every human being has. It affects the deepest part of a person, the "spirit," however God is recognized or defined, and even if he is denied.

For several years after Vatican Council II, the rapid rise and fall of theories and movements of spirituality kept many Catholics ill at ease with their prayer life. The genuine developments were not always much more helpful than the erratic. The liturgical revival, in making worship more communal, sometimes failed to allow for the private and devotional; awareness of the needs of the secular city brought emphasis on the social consequences of the gospel, but cast doubt on other good consequences.

Nervousness in religious matters is something new for Catholics. The lines of spiritual doctrine used to be closely drawn. Every Catholic writer drew from the same philosophical and theological pool of terms and interpretations. It was immediately evident, even without the imprimatur stamped inside, whether a book was Catholic or not.

Some would say it was better that way, and safer. One thing is sure: the uniformity of Catholic theological and spiritual writing before Vatican II made inevitable the shock Catholics experienced in its wake. We were not accustomed to deal with a variety of religious opinions and therefore, as during the days of uniformity, people open to new things tended to act on the latest religious book or theological fad without subjecting it to scrutiny. The effects were often disastrous.

The turmoil in Catholic spirituality in the late Sixties left a fallout of mistrust of "new" or different ideas in theology and spirituality. The more the Thirties, Forties and Fifties receded into the past, the more they became glazed over with an aura of peace and joy and holiness. Catholics with this nostalgia took refuge in the Tridentine Mass, in their grade school catechisms, and even in older English translations of the Bible. Critical hesitance is good, but this suspicion of modern religious thought has become an extreme among some Catholics. It even led some out of the Church.

The mainstream Catholic, however, is still engaged in a responsible search for stable and reliable foundations of spirituality for this new age. He is driven down underneath the shifting surface to the bedrock: the foundational documents, the Scriptures of the Old and New Testaments. This book is meant to help in that search for reliable norms by developing the biblical message of spirituality in the light of the Church's authentic teaching in Vatican Council II.

We know well enough that the Bible does not give us a code of ethics. It is not a collection of rules and maxims, a "way" in the sense of some religious writings of the East. We would also be mistaken to expect the Bible to furnish the specific guidance of a devotional manual. The biblical program of spirituality is a call to arms, precise at times, but not casuistic: repent, believe, return to the Lord, listen to his word, follow him.

The theme that binds all the biblical instructions and injunctions about human living into a unity is that of God's call and man's response. A person defines himself before God in his reaction to divine revelation, however and wherever it is expressed to him. This biblical concept of spirituality establishes the pattern of this book. Man's response to God's word determines his relationship to God and his own spiritual identity. Spirituality, in biblical terms, is responding to the word of God.

RESPONDING TO THE WORD

CHAPTER ONE

THE WORD OF GOD

As children of our time, we automatically think first of the word of God as a written book, the Bible. Surrounded as we are daily by oceans of print, word has come more and more to mean for us what appears on a printed page. Marshall McLuhan may be right in saying that the written word will not mean much to us in the future, but it determines our thinking now. We rely on newspapers and books for information, on signed contracts to seal transactions, on letters and memos to express our thoughts. We communicate by speech, too, but not like our preliterate ancestors. To break my word does not mean, as it did for them, to break myself. "Speech" and "talk" express oral communication for us, but "word" can be something written down. The word of God is more often than not equated with the written Bible.

The Bible is the word of God, of course, but that is not all there is to it. The meaning of word of God in Scripture reaches beyond the pages of any book, even the Bible. The word of God is not first of all something written down. The biblical authors describe it as a saving power or force let loose in the world, an *event* of salvation. The "word of God to Israel" in Peter's speech at Cornelius' house (Ac 10:36) is everything that Jesus did, beginning with his baptism in the Jordan. The word may be Jesus himself or the good news of forgiveness he brings; it may be the proclamation of the kingdom of God, or the cross and resurrection: the word is the Christ-event.

The word of God is no mere oracle, no revelation in the narrow sense of interpretation of the mysterious. It is a force let loose in the world, creating, redeeming, judging. Believers speak of the "good news of the kingdom" (Mt 4:23), "the gospel of God's grace" (Ac 20:24), "the glad tidings of salvation" (Ep 1:13). St. Paul's rich salvation vocabulary includes: "the word of life" (Ph 2:16), "the message of the cross" (1 Cor 1:18), "the message of reconciliation" (2 Cor 5:19), "the word of faith" (Rm 10:8). The person of Christ and his message are never very far apart in these phrases. In the First Letter of John, "the word of life" may mean the message of salvation, the salvation-life, the Savior, or all these together (1:1-2). The active power of the word of God is expressed especially in the image of the two-edged sword. The word cuts both ways, saving and judging. It is "living and effective . . . ; penetrates and divides soul and spirit, joints and marrow" (Heb 4:12). The Christian warrior wields the sword of the spirit, the word of God (Ep 6:17).

A Powerful Word

The background for such a concept of "word" has to be sought in the Hebrew vocabulary and ways of thinking which underlie the Greek text of the New Testament. The Hebrew term *dabar* covers the meanings of "event" and "thing" as well as "word." We get the flavor of this in Luke's infancy narrative: "Let us go over to Bethlehem and see this *word* that has taken place" (Lk 2:15). Abraham's military exploits against the four Eastern kings are "words" (Gn 15:1). Isaac's servant describes "all the words he had done" in finding Rebekah (Gn 24:66). To

the Old Testament believer, the most important words of
God are the great events of salvation, especially Exodus
and the Covenant. But there is an even more significant
difference between Hebrew and Western concepts of
word. Word expresses not only a meaning or an idea, but
in Hebrew involves a dynamic element as well. The word,
and not only the speaker, is somehow active. A word is
"lying" if what is stated or promised does not happen.
A thought must be expressed and a statement must take
flesh in deed to qualify as a word in the full sense. There
is a subtle feeling that the power of a spoken word can be
somehow drained away when the word is written on
paper.

So strong is the spoken word that once uttered it is
treated as having an existence independent of the speaker.
Isaac was heartbroken by his mistake in giving the blessing
of the firstborn to the conniving Jacob, but he could not
bring the blessing back. Esau had to be patient with a
second-rate blessing (Gn 27:30-40). The prophet Balaam
was hired to curse the Israelites but the word put into his
mouth by the Lord was a word of blessing (Nb 23:11-12).
A woman accused of adultery was made to drink "water
of bitterness" containing a curse washed off a scroll by
the priest. If she was guilty, the curse would attack her
entrails, but if innocent, she would be unharmed (Nb
5:12-28).

If man's word is so powerful, how much more powerful and effective is the word of God. Its effect among men
is compared to the life-giving energy of water on the
parched earth:

> Just as from the heavens the rain and snow come down
> And do not return there till they have watered the
>   earth, making it fertile and fruitful,
> Giving seed to him who sows and bread
>   to him who eats,

So shall my word be that goes forth from my mouth;
It shall not return to me void, but shall do my will,
     achieving the end for which I sent it.
                              (Is 55:10-11).

This word can be compared to a two-edged sword
which connot be staved off or blunted. It saves or it
judges. The judging word is like a hammer shattering rock
(Jr 23:29). The word is creative. In the first creation
account in Genesis, God is not seen; only his voice is heard.
But that is enough: "Let there be light; and there was
light" (1:3). The psalms celebrate this creative power of
God's word: "By the word of the Lord the heavens were
made; by the breath of his mouth all their host" (Ps 33:6).

The Lord entrusts his powerful word to his messengers,
the prophets, men chosen to speak for him to the people.
Their vocation does not depend on talent or training or
even a feeling for the task. Amos and Micah were un-
educated. Moses and Jeremiah begged to be overlooked.
But when they did accept, the accounts say, the word of
the Lord *came* to them, gripped them wholly and changed
their lives. The experience was like having your lips seared
by a coal from the heavenly altar (Is 6:6-7), and finding
a burning fire shut up in your bones (Jer 20:9). The
priests found the word proclaimed by Amos "too heavy
for the land to bear," but he warned that a famine of the
word of God would make the people stagger even more
(Am 7:10; 8:11-12).

The Word is a Seed

The word of God never *comes* to Jesus in the New
Testament, as it did to the prophets and to John the Baptist (Lk 3:2), because Jesus *is* the word of God made
flesh (Jn 1:14), the Father's "last word" in a long series
of pronouncements (Heb 1:1-2). As the Word, he is

God's saving and judging presence in person. His message and the early community's preaching about him are also the word of God, packed with the power of salvation. Where Christ appears, the salvation of God is at work, the kingdom comes for the whole man: ". . . the blind recover their sight, cripples walk, lepers are cured, the deaf hear, dead men are raised to life, and the poor have the good news preached to them" (Lk 7:22).

Picking up an Old Testament image, Jesus compared the word of God to the seed sown by a farmer. It falls on the footpath, on rocky ground and among thorns to no avail, but in fertile soil it produces a vast harvest (Mk 4:3-9). The word of God, like the seed, has the power of life in itself. Its lifegiving energy does not depend on the preacher or the listener, but it is only the listener who can provide the soil for growth.

This keeps the power of the word from being magic. There is saving power in every act of Jesus, but it is not magical power. Jesus worked many miracles, but always in a context of faith. When he found no faith at Nazareth, "he could work no miracles there" (Mk 6:5). The sacraments contain divine power, but no automatic effect. Nothing happens except condemnation where there is no disposition (1 Cor 11:29). Paul thanks God for the faith of the Thessalonians, which made it possible for the word to go to work in them (1 Th 2:13). It was not the same for some of the Israelites in the desert: "The word which they heard did not profit them, for they did not receive it in faith" (Heb 4:2).

Paul is aware that the power of his ministry comes from the word of God and not from himself. Usually so intent upon making his message clear and unmistakable, he sometimes speaks bluntly and without explanation to impress upon his listeners the origin of the saving power in their midst:

> When I came to you I did not come proclaiming God's testimony with any particular eloquence or "wisdom." . . . My message and preaching had none of the persuasive force of "wise" argumentation, but the convincing power of the Spirit. As a consequence, your faith rests not on the wisdom of men but on the power of God (1 Cor 2:1-5).

Where is the Word?

Confronted with the marvels of this richly powerful word, the natural reaction is "Where do I find this word?" The answer: everywhere. God is always speaking to his children. The Book of Deuteronomy put it beautifully in speaking of God's gift of the Law:

> It is not up in the sky, that you should say, "Who will go up in the sky to get it for us and tell us of it, that we may carry it out?" Nor is it across the sea, that you should say, "Who will cross the sea to get it for us and tell us of it, that we may carry it out?" No, it is something very near to you, already in your mouths and in your hearts; you have only to carry it out (Dt 30:12-14).

God's communication with man is a vital force in each life. Vatican II aimed at recovering the vitality of this dialogue between God and man in its teaching on revelation. The strong stress on authentic doctrine in the Catholic tradition led us in the past almost to equate revelation with the content of the Church's teaching. In this way of thinking, the "source" of revelation is a deposit of truths in Scripture and tradition, to which the Church, as the divinely authorized interpreter, has the key. At Vatican II the first great debate concerned whether or not to speak of "two sources" of revelation in Scripture and tradition. As a result of Pope John's dramatic intervention the Council spoke rather of Jesus Christ as the one source of revelation, with Scripture and tradition proclaiming or transmitting this word.

The Council's teaching on revelation is expressed most thoroughly in the decree *Dei Verbum*.

> In his goodness and wisdom, God chose to reveal himself and to make known to us the hidden purpose of his will by which through Christ, the Word made flesh, man has access to the Father in the Holy Spirit and comes to share in the divine nature. Through this revelation, therefore, the invisible God out of the abundance of his love speaks to men as friends and lives among them, so that he may invite and take them into fellowship with himself (no. 2).

Revelation is taken out of the category of written documents and presented as personal and dynamic. It is as Father, not as a teacher or lawgiver, that God above all reveals himself to us. His revelation is his gift of himself. God our Father has spoken and is now speaking to us, and the primary truth communicated is God himself.

What does this mean for the individual child of this loving Father? It means that he is revealing himself to me personally at every moment, in whatever happens to me and in everything I do. He is in my work and relaxation, in the sharing with people I live with and meet during any day. He may communicate powerfully with me even through some joy or tragedy. Or he may reach me best at a time of prayer. Every time I let his word into my life, his power goes to work in me. I grow by the power of the word.

The Bible as God's Word

Though the word of God unleashes its saving power wherever it is uttered, the holy Scripture is a privileged source of this word. God speaks in the midst of every person's life, in every honest search for truth, in every expression of human beauty and truth; he speaks in art, music, in literature. Except in Scripture, though, there is always an admixture of the word of man, fallible and unreliable. The Bible is the full and faithful reflection of God's revelation and serves as the touchstone for what is the word of God in our world and what is not. Written under the inspiration of the Holy Spirit, the Bible needs interpretation by the living Church, also under the inspiration of the Spirit. When we read this word in faith and "in the Church" (*Sacrosanctum Concilium*, no. 7). we know by God's own guarantee of biblical inspiration that we are in touch with the saving word of God. As soon as this contact takes place, the word of God begins changing our hearts, transforming us into Christ.

The Church Fathers bore witness to this inherent power of the word in the biblical writings. The ancient Church loved this healing and transforming power of the Lord in Scripture. St. Jerome said "Not to know Scripture is not to know Christ," and compared the Bible to the Eucharistic Body of Christ. St. Augustine spoke of the "sacraments of Scripture" and St. Benedict of the "medicines of Scripture."

The bishops of Vatican II were harking back to this patristic reverence when they called the Scriptures and the Eucharist two sources of the same bread of life, and drew attention to the great force and power for salvation in the biblical word:

> Inspired by God and committed once and for all to writing, the Scriptures impart the word of God himself without change, and make the voice of the Holy Spirit resound in the words of the prophets and apostles. Therefore, like the Christian religion itself, all the preaching of the Church must be nourished and

ruled by sacred Scripture. For in the sacred books, the Father who is in heaven meets his children with great love and speaks with them; and the force and power in the word of God is so great that it remains the support and energy of the Church, the strength of faith for her children, the food of the soul, the pure and perennial source of spiritual life (*Dei Verbum,* no. 21).

They further urged Catholic believers to renew the Church at its heart by forming close personal relationships with the biblical word, depending on it as a basis for faith and prayer.

When I read in faith what Paul wrote to the Corinthians about Christian love, my own understanding and insight may initiate reflection and an inner change of direction. Any sensitive human writing can set such a renewal in motion. But because this reading is Sacred Scripture, there is more. God's power is at work in this word to change me from selfishness to service. The Bible thus makes God present to the believer in the infinite variation of his message. The word saving and forming believers through the sacramental life of the Church becomes more precise and personal here. The Bible is a prism refracting God's word to the corners of my life, now through a psalm, now in a prophetic oracle, now by the story of the man born blind. Because of this, the Bible is set apart from other spiritual writings, however moving or profound.

A story from the desert Fathers brings this point home. A young man came to one of the old hermits and made his request: "Father, I want to seek God in this wilderness, too. How can I become a holy monk?" "My son, go over into one of those caves, taking with you this Book of holy Scriptures. Read it day and night and you will find what you are seeking." After three days, the young man returned, complaining that the reading was boring, that his mind wandered, and that he remembered little of what he read. "Do not despair, my son. You are doing fine. But do this also. Fill a basket with sand and set it just outside your cave. Every morning and evening pour a bucket of water over the sand. Come back in a week and we will talk." The young monk followed the old man's strange instructions. At the end of the week he still complained about his lack of progress in holy reading. "But about the sand, every time I pour water over it, some leaks out the sides of the basket." This same simple process continued, with the young monk coming each week to talk with his spiritual father. Finally he reported: "Father, the sand is all gone. For the past two days I have been pouring water into a clean basket. But with the reading, I find myself just as lazy and bored and forgetful as ever." The old man rose. "My son, you are the basket. The sand is your sinfulness, the water is the word of God. The basket doesn't remember the water that gradually cleansed it. No more do you remember every word of Holy Scripture that you read. But if you continue to pour the water of God's word over your sinfulness every day, some day you will be clean."

READING SUGGESTIONS

Vatican Council II, *Constitution on Divine Revelation (Dei Verbum)*.

Jones, Alexander. *God's Living Word*. Glen Rock, N. J.: Deus Books, 1965.

Martin, George. *Reading Scripture as the Word of God*. Ann Arbor: Word of Life, 1975.

Stuhlmueller, Carroll. *The Prophets and the Word of God*. Notre Dame: Fides, 1964.

CHAPTER TWO

THE UNPREDICTABLE GOD

The powerful word of God meets us everywhere, creating, saving, healing, judging. Our investigation into the meaning of the word of God has already told us something about the kind of God who speaks this word. But the deeper our knowledge of God the better prepared we are to listen and respond to the word he utters.

Knowledge of God is twofold: first there is the personal knowledge of love, beyond words and descriptions. This is the essential knowledge, the knowledge that is eternal life (Jn 17:3). But there is also doctrinal knowledge, knowing who God is through study of his self-revelation given to us in the inspired Scriptures. All doctrine is dry straw without the personal love-knowledge. But doctrine can deepen the foundation of this love and direct it to the true God rather than to some idol created by a misguided imagination. The next two chapters will search the Scriptures to strengthen our knowledge of the God whose word calls us continually to life.

A Hidden God

It may come as a surprise to find out that the God bent on revealing himself to man is described as a "hidden God" (Is 45:15). His very hiddenness, it turns out, is part of his identity. We may be annoyed that God does not tell us everything about himself, but the Hebrews did not find it strange. For them, it was surprising that he spoke at all. Yahweh is so different from man and far above him that to hear his voice or to look on his face is to die (Ex 20:18-21). Moses, his closest co-worker, asked to see the divine glory. Yahweh agreed but took necessary precautions. Moses could only glimpse the back of God as he walked away (Ex 33:18-23).

One way the Bible expresses this hiddenness and otherness of God is by calling him "holy." This stresses the glory and majesty of God, his distance from the frailty of man. The seraphim in Isaiah's Temple vision cried out, "Holy, holy, holy is the Lord of hosts! All the earth is filled with his glory!" The Temple shook and was filled with smoke. Isaiah knew he was teetering on the threshold between life and death. "Woe is me, I am doomed! For I am a man of unclean lips, living among a people of unclean lips; yet my eyes have seen the King, the Lord of hosts!" (Is 6:3-5). In the Sinai story this otherness of God is expressed by the smoke, thunder and lightning, and by the danger of even touching the mountain where God will appear. Yahweh appears in the midst of forces man cannot adequately understand or harness (Ex 19: 16-25). Moses had been introduced to this God at the burning bush, where he was told, "Come no nearer! Remove the sandals from your feet, for the place where you stand is holy ground" (Ex 3:5).

Modern readers are scandalized by the story of Uzzah, the Israelite who was struck dead when he reached out to steady the Ark of the Covenant (the seat of God's presence) when it seemed in danger of falling (2 S 6: 3-7). The story does not say Uzzah sinned in so acting— his intentions were good—but that he was not qualified to touch the Ark. He had not been consecrated for this function. The story instills a reverential fear of the hidden holy Yahweh.

The hiddenness of God is expressed also in reverence for his name. In ancient thought a person's name was not merely a mark of identification. It was deeply part of him. The name revealed the person. God could not be forced to tell his name, that is, reveal himself (Gn 32:30; Jg 13:17-18), but he did reveal it in his own good time to Moses (Ex 3:13-15). The people needed to know the name of Yahweh to experience the assurance and protection it signified.

A God Who Speaks

The hiddenness of God is, of course, not the whole story. He is a hidden God who reveals himself to his people. This, in a nutshell, is what causes the trouble. The Lord is far away but he is near: He is paradoxical and unpredictable. The same Old Testament documents which show concern for God's distance and superiority display him speaking with men and involving himself directly in their affairs. He kept the people from touching the mountain, but spoke with Moses and gave him a message for the people.

The prophets of Israel stress the nearness of the Lord to his people. These are his spokesmen, his intimates. They are entrusted with the word of God to wield it like a sword among men. It is their duty and privilege to make the hidden God known among the people, to reveal his intentions. Nothing could be more devastating than a famine of this word (Am 8:11-12). The account of the vocation of Isaiah combines graphically the distance and nearness of Yahweh. He is holy and transcendent, but he asks "Whom shall I send? Who will go for us?", and commits his word to the prophet (Is 6:1-9).

The hiddenness of God, then, does not compromise his intention to reveal. But it serves as a corrective to human attempts to discern God's purpose without his willing it.

In biblical revelation, God always has the initiative. No one can go up to heaven to draw his word down. Man is not to seek to uncover the will of God by divination and necromancy (Dt 18:9-14). The neighbors of Israel erred in making gods in their own image, and to avoid a similar mistake, Israel is prohibited from making images of Yahweh (Ex 20:4). The Lord has promised to be with his people always: no need to keep him handy on the shelf. The men who made the idols could define them, completely identify them, think and speak for them. Yahweh is a God who speaks for himself. It is God's speaking (in the sense of his self-revelation) that makes us realize that he is personal, a living God. The gods of the idolmakers are dumb. The god of philosophy is a deduction from premises, incapable of surprise. But Yahweh is a living God, unique and personal, a mystery.

A God of Mystery

We can know Yahweh because he gives himself to us. He draws us into his acquaintance by speaking to us, by acting on us. The irony is that the God who speaks is even more mysterious than the one who remains silent. The more we know of him, the more we don't know. Every new act requires an adjustment of the picture we had drawn. Our knowledge of this revealing God is like our developing knowledge of human persons.

It is easy for us to categorize persons we know very faintly. We can give thumbnail descriptions of political figures, distant churchmen, movie stars, sports personalities. But we find ourselves groping for words to describe members of our own family, close friends, members of our religious community. They cannot be summed up in a sentence or two because we know them too well to overlook the complexity and richness of their personhood.

Though we imitate God by revealing ourselves to one

another in word and deed, there are obvious differences. Human persons never fully understand themselves, so the self-disclosure is often distorted. We do not have complete control over the revelation even of what we know about ourselves. We unwittingly reveal what we would prefer to keep hidden, and obscure what we want to express. But God knows himself perfectly and is in complete command of his self-revelation. His words and deeds are not accidents. He shows more and more that he is supremely individual, "his own person." He cannot be deduced from principles, and will continually slip out from under the premises set up for him. There is always more to our God than meets the eye.

Elijah learned this when he was down and out, running away from his hopeless mission and wanting to die. Yahweh came to him where he was hiding in a cave on Mount Horeb. He told the prophet to await the divine manifestation. It was then that Elijah, the know-it-all, found out how impossible it is to predict the Lord and his ways. Elijah knew from religious tradition and past experience that the Lord always appeared in the terrible magnificence of wind, earthquake and fire. But wind, earthquake and fire came and went without the appearance of the Lord. It was in the gentle breeze, against all the rules, that Yahweh came (1 K 19:9-13).

An Unpredictable God

The God of our fathers has always been like this. He is an unpredictable God. We have permitted the philosophers to lull us into the assurance that we know more about God and his operations than we really do, but the God of the Scriptures is a puzzle. He has a penchant for paradox. He is continually doing things his own way, appearing where men least expect him, and acting without regard for convention and human wisdom. He expresses his saving

will according to his own preferences (or whims), show-
ing himself supremely independent. A deistic god, aloof
in his own realm, makes much more sense than a God
who lets himself become entangled in the ups and downs
of human history. The God of Scripture opens himself
wide to embarrassment.

Even if, for the sake of argument, a self-respecting
deity had accepted the principle of historical involvement,
he would scarcely have approved the choice of a small,
hardly identifiable nation like Israel. The powers in Meso-
potamia and Egypt were much better equipped than Israel
to convince the world of divine judgment. It would have
been at least logical, once the principle of historical involvement was in force, for God to become the official
deity of a powerful nation. But Yahweh chose Israel. There
is no way to account for this election except by attributing
it, as Yahweh did himself, to the free choice of his love
(Dt 7:7-8). Men have always balked at the choice, and
anti-Semitism is an enduring sign of the inability to acknowledge the fact that "Salvation is from the Jews" (Jn
4:22).

Yahweh enmeshed himself in the history of a single
human family in order to show his love to all men. Abraham was one of many caravaners in the Fertile Crescent
around the year 1800 B.C. The promise was to be carried
on through his family descent, and properly through the
firstborn sons. The biblical accounts emphasize the inse-
curity and uncertainty of this particular lineage. God
chose to bind his promise to the patriarchal heir, and then
picked a family notorious for the unreliability of its male
issue.

Over and over again Yahweh surprises by breaking
away from human convention. By a remarkable intervention, a son is born to the elderly Abraham and Sarah. This
son is given the name Isaac, which Genesis uses to indicate

the surprise or the playfulness of God (from the verb meaning "to laugh"—Gn 21:1-7). But the relief of having a son is short-lived. Isaac is scarcely given and he is demanded back in sacrifice, a dramatic test of faith and an instruction to readers that the plan of God may be carried out any way God wishes.

Once God aligns himself to a human dynasty, he could be expected to follow the rules, especially since they seem to be his own rules. But Yahweh does not. "My thoughts are not your thoughts, nor are your ways my ways, says the Lord" (Is 55:8). Among Isaac's children, the bearer of the promise turns out to be not Esau, the firstborn and rightful heir, but Jacob, the younger brother, a liar and a sneak. Among the sons of Jacob, it is not Reuben but Joseph, the next-to-youngest, who saves the family from extinction.

The campaign against Jericho prospers through the good will of a prostitute. Samuel, anointer of kings, is the son of a woman despised because of her sterility. David is the youngest of eight sons; his choice is a source of amazement (1 S 16:5-13). The prophets are God's spokesmen and should be eager, dynamic and forceful. But some of the most important are fearful and hesitant. Moses and Jeremiah protest that they cannot speak. Amos and Micah preach at the religious centers without any special preparation to make their mission effective. God's choice defies man's logic.

The people wondered why, with God in control, their nation did not achieve an ever-spiralling prosperity. The kingdom of David was a moment of national grandeur, but it was only a moment. Already under his son Solomon, frayed edges began to show. After Solomon, the people were split into two kingdoms (1 K 12). Something of the wealth and power of David's time began to grow again in the Northern Kingdom of Israel. But it was precisely at the zenith of this growth that Israel fell to Sargon of Assyria and the worldly kingdom was destroyed (2 K 17). Judah to the South gloated over the fall of its rival, but within two hundred years Judah was also overrun and its people exiled in Babylon (2 K 25). All these tragedies could be interpreted as signs of the weakness of the God of the Hebrews. Many of the people fell for this and threw in their lot with the god of Babylon.

Judah returned from the Exile as had been foretold by her prophets, but again the outcome was not exactly as the prophets had foreseen. The return was anything but glorious. Only a remnant would struggle through the rebuilding of the Temple and the resettling of the land. The new kingdom didn't burst forth in new growth and splendor. That was not to be the way Yahweh's power would be shown. Judah barely held its own in the world, and by the time of Jesus' birth was under foreign domination.

The Exodus

We need to go back for a moment to an event skimmed over in this speeding narrative of Old Testament history. The Exodus was the saving word of Yahweh to his people. It was the momentous deliverance that gave every other event meaning for the Hebrew people. When they were hopelessly down and out, struggling for their very lives in slavery to Pharaoh, Yahweh reached into their midst with his "strong hand and outstretched arm" (Dt 4:34). They were not even really a people yet. He made them a people by his love.

The action of God was a stroke out of the blue. The birth of Moses and his call illustrate the unexpected in the divine deliverance. He was barely saved from death in infancy. After a frustrated attempt to get involved for the good of his people, Moses retired to the quiet life of a shepherd in a distant land. It was well after he had settled into this shepherd life, when he was eighty years old, that the call of the Lord came.

Moses wasn't prepared to answer the call and neither were the people. They listened to the Lord grudgingly. The burning bush upset Moses' tranquillity. As he listened to the voice and realized what was happening, he saw his peaceful shepherd's existence begin slipping away. The stirring announcement of Yahweh had little effect on him: "I have come down to rescue my people from the hands of the Egyptians and lead them out of that land into a good and spacious land, a land flowing with milk and honey" (Ex 3:8). Moses only thinks of excuses: "Who am I that I should go? . . . What if they ask me your name? . . . Suppose they will not believe me? . . . I am slow of speech and tongue." The answer of Yahweh is simple. "I will be with you." Eventually Moses realized that that was all he needed. The Lord would deliver his people in his own good way and time and with power to spare. Moses had only to be his willing instrument.

The people were not ready either. At first, they believed and bowed in worship when they heard of the coming deliverance (Ex 4:31); and they watched in awe as Yahweh stunned Pharaoh by the series of plagues. But their real feelings began to show when they lost the security of their slavery and headed for the Red Sea and the desert with the Egyptians in pursuit. "Were there no burial places in Egypt that you had to bring us out here to die in the desert? Why did you do this to us? Why did you bring us out of Egypt?" (Ex 14:11). The Lord knew well the cowardice and fickleness of his people. He had re-routed them to the sea in the first place so that they would not have to fight, for "They might change their minds and return to Egypt" (13:17). Even after the undeniable show of might in the crossing of the Sea, the Israelites were pessimistic and fearful. The Books of Exodus and Numbers stress the murmuring of the people in the desert.

There is a moment in the narrative, though, when Moses and the people realize what is happening and rejoice in the divine love demonstrated in the mighty act of deliverance. Standing on the bank on the far side of the Red Sea, they look back across to the land of slavery, their eyes searching the waters for any sign of their unhappy pursuers.

> I will sing to the Lord, for he is gloriously triumphant;
>   horse and chariot he has cast into the sea.
> My strength and my courage is the Lord,
>   and he has been my savior.
> He is my God, I praise him;
>   the God of my father, I extol him (Ex 15:1-2).

The deliverance of Exodus, where God showed his love in surprising ways, became the symbol for all other divine acts of salvation in Israel.

The Unpredictable Son

The unpredictability of God climaxes in the event of the incarnation. God becomes man. And in the case of Jesus it is like father, like son. The fulfillment of the ages does not emerge from the leading priestly families of Jerusalem. He is born to an obscure maid from Nazareth. He is a carpenter's son with a controversial family background. When he begins to be identified for what he is, Jesus rejects the political messiahship the Jews were preparing for him. He will not be a king in the image of David the mighty, but will preach a kingdom in which the key to success is humble service and suffering.

Many were confused, even one as well-versed in prophecy as John the Baptist. After having brought Jesus to the attention of the multitudes, John had second thoughts while he languished in prison. He had depicted a harsh messianic preacher who would lay the axe to the roots and apply stiff penalties for sin (Lk 3:7-9). Word reached him that Jesus was taking a softer approach, proclaiming God's love for sinners and forgiveness for everyone. John sent two of his own followers to find out whether Jesus was the one they were waiting for or not. Jesus defends his ministry in words from the Old Testament prophecies and then issues a promise that is also a warning to anyone who rejects the divine plan because it does not measure up to human expectation: "Happy is the man who does not find me a stumbling block" (Lk 7:18-23). Man must adapt himself to the revelation of God in Jesus, not the other way around.

Jesus is no more careful about choosing his closest co-workers than Yahweh was in choosing his prophets. Jesus does not search far afield for the most qualified, but takes men who happen to be at hand, rough fishermen from his own Galilee. We might have preferred the sensible Andrew to be the leader of the Twelve, but Jesus picks his brother, Simon Peter, the most irrepressible of the group. Peter acts and speaks before he thinks a problem through, bringing embarrassment to himself and to Jesus. He is not the convincing, single-minded leader one would appoint to head a movement.

There are hotheads like James and John and there are the cynical like Thomas and Nathaniel. There is a traitor. If Jesus was trying to give his group a reputation for patriotism and respectability, he did not promote the cause by choosing Simon the Zealot, whose title indicates affiliation with a revolutionary activity against Rome. Jewish tempers, on the other side, must have been aroused by the presence of the tax collector, Matthew, who symbolized the hated control of Rome.

Jesus did not force people into belief by the convincing clarity of his words and deeds. Some were impressed by his parables and miracles, others could scoff. Jesus' manner of life seemed to follow no strict pattern. Sometimes he broke with legal requirements and sometimes he observed them. Sometimes he hid from his enemies, sometimes he faced them. He consorted with all types of sinners and outcasts, saying that it is the poor, not the rich, who are close to the kingdom of God. He said it is not the external observance that counts, but the internal attitude, so that you can't say for sure who is holy. He claimed that God does not judge by human standards, so that the eleventh-hour arrival might receive as much as the all-day worker.

To the chagrin of his followers Jesus went to death, and then, most unexpected of all, he appeared to them alive after death. Nothing in Jewish thought had prepared them for an eschatological victory before the end of history. Many couldn't believe it, and those who did needed a long time to make sense of it. Then instead of consolidating the kingdom, Jesus ceased being visibly present among his followers. He sent the mysterious Holy Spirit, who breathes where he wills and is God's unpredictability in person. In a saying that became a favorite of New Testament authors, Jesus compared his coming back to the attack of a "thief in the night" (Mt 24:43). God appears when and where men least expect him. He acts in ways they cannot foresee or understand. He is an unpredictable God.

READING SUGGESTIONS

Arias, Juan. *The God I Don't Believe In*. St. Meinrad, Ind.: Abbey Press, 1973.

Evely, Louis. *That Man is You*. Westminster, Md.: Newman Press, 1964.

Jensen, Joseph. *God's Word to Israel*. Boston: Allyn and Bacon, 1968.

Sontag, Frederick. *The God of Evil*. New York: Harper and Row, 1970.

CHAPTER THREE

THE LOVING GOD

The Scriptural review of the preceding chapter could leave the impression that the God of our fathers is only a player of games, a prankster. If he is so thoroughly unpredictable, how can we know anything certain about him? But to say Yahweh is unpredictable is not to say he is unprincipled. He is playful but not capricious. There is method in his madness.

The God of Israel, unlike the gods of Israel's neighbors, has a purpose. This has always distinguished Yahweh from the other gods. The pagan gods were enmeshed in nature and in history, not really in control of them. To reach the god you had to join the cycle of nature and history in a ritual mime. Nature revolved in the seasons; history was a recurring circle, going nowhere in particular. Divine activity manifested itself in the repetition of displays of might and power. Single actions meant nothing, but if notable historical events (wars, accession of kings) or cosmic spectacles (spring rebirth, earthquakes) were repeated regularly enough, the presence of divinity could be assumed.

Under Yahweh's lordship, however, history is not a circle but a straight line moving toward a goal. The important events are not those that recur, but those that occur only once but magnificently, like the Exodus and the Resurrection. The Lord is not unprincipled at all. He has revealed the purpose behind everything he does. The mighty deeds of Yahweh are not intended to show off his power but to demonstrate his love. This is something men never dreamed of. Yahweh reveals himself as a loving God, a God who cares for his people, cares to the point of sending his own Son as our redeemer. God is predictable in his love. It is this that we can always depend on. We do not know what our God will do next, but we know that whatever he does will be an act of love.

God is Love

The word used by the Old Testament to describe this quality in Yahweh is *hesed*. This expresses God's "tender loving care" for his people. Often it is linked with *emeth* and *emunah*, words indicating truth, faithfulness, steadfastness. The God of the covenant is a God of faithful love.

> The Lord, the Lord, a merciful and gracious God, slow to anger and rich in kindness (*hesed*) and fidelity (*emeth*), continuing his kindness for a thousand generations (Ex 34:6-7).

To know Yahweh's name is to be convinced of his unfailing presence and love. This is the answer Moses got, and it was all he needed (Ex 3:12-17).

The most stirring Old Testament statement of God's loving faithfulness is in the Book of Hosea. Yahweh is the faithful husband married to unfaithful Israel. Though Israel sins again and again in going after other lovers, Yahweh does not disown her. He is there to take her back when she has stopped sinning.

> I will espouse you to me forever;
> I will espouse you in right and in justice,
>   in love and in mercy;

I will espouse you in fidelity,
>   and you shall know the Lord (Hos 2:21-22).

Later the prophet changes the image to that of parent and child. Yahweh is a father or mother with a troublesome son. We are taken inside Yahweh's mind and pace the floor with him as he debates with himself over his treatment of the miscreant Israel (Ephraim).

When Israel was a child I loved him,
>   out of Egypt I called my son.
The more I called them,
>   the farther they went from me.
Sacrificing to the Baals
>   and burning incense to idols.
Yet it was I who taught Ephraim to walk,
>   who took them in my arms;
I drew them with human cords,
>   with bands of love;
I fostered them like one
>   who raises an infant to his cheeks;
Yet, though I stooped to feed my child,
>   they did not know that I was their healer (11:1-4).

The response of Israel to this love has been shameless, unforgivable. Israel has not behaved like a true son of Yahweh; he has brought disgrace on Yahweh, made him seem a fool. And so Yahweh vows to let Israel be destroyed as he deserves:

He shall return to the land of Egypt,
>   and Assyria shall be his king;
The sword shall begin with his cities
>   and end by consuming his solitudes (11:5-6).

Yahweh has vented his righteous anger. But he cannot disown his son. And so, against all reason, Yahweh vows to continue showering his love on the ungrateful Israel. He refuses to repay in kind the heartless rejection of the one he loves.

> How could I give you up, O Ephraim,
>> or deliver you up, O Israel? . . .
> My heart is overwhelmed,
>> my pity is stirred.
> I will not give vent to my blazing anger,
>> I will not destroy Ephraim again;
> For I am God and not man,
>> the Holy One present among you;
> I will not let the flames consume you (11:8-9).

This is the God of Scripture, a God of extravagant love. "I am God and not man." Yahweh is above our narrow vindictiveness; he is free to love a person without demanding love or good conduct in return. Everything our God does, and the only thing he does, is love, for "God is love" (1 Jn 4, 8). "Though the mountains leave their place and the hills be shaken, my love shall never leave you nor my covenant of peace with you be shaken" (Is 54:10).

Jesus

The ultimate revelation of this love of God comes to us in human form. Jesus is the incarnate love of God. The covenant virtues *hesed* and *emeth* (love and truth) become visible most dramatically in his life. "The Word became flesh and made his dwelling among us, and we have seen his glory: the glory of an only Son coming from the Father, filled with enduring love" (Jn 1:14). Jesus does not spare himself. His life is for others, to be given as a ransom for the many (Mk 10:45). In his ministry, Jesus looks especially for those who are helpless and hopeless. He shows they are loved. His death is the conclusive proof of God's love for us. He died for us while we were still in our sins (Rm 5:5-8).

Jesus teaches us to call God our Father. He gives us the special name for God he uses himself—Abba—a name so intimate that no one dared use it before. And in the story of the prodigal son, Jesus removed all doubt about the extravagance of God's love. "While he was still a long way off, his father caught sight of him and was deeply moved. He ran out to meet him, threw his arms around his neck, and kissed him" (Lk 15:20). It has been said that the most important turning point in a person's life is when he experiences God not as Creator or Judge but as Father.

Jesus speaks to sinners of forgiveness. He brings good news: your sins are forgiven, you may now go in peace. Be free of your past, of what drags you down. Be healed. He tells us of a God whose love is continually creative and imaginative, always finding new ways to free from sin and fear. "Fear not, little flock, for it has pleased your Father to give you the kingdom" (Lk 12:32). Francis Thompson described this God as the Hound of Heaven, following relentlessly in his love.

The God of Our Life

The love of God revealed in Jesus is the constant word spoken powerfully in each of our lives. The love is always there but we do not always know how to recognize it. God's predictable love, we have seen, is expressed in ways that are unpredictable from our point of view. This is precisely the test. Can we live with this unpredictable, purposeful God? Dealing with him does not follow the familiar patterns of human relationships. We cannot judge the motives of God the way we judge the motives of man. God has only one motive.

How does one get along with this remarkable God? What is the secret in managing for the moment and in planning for the future? Probably the significance of this question is best underscored by first approaching its opposite: How would one live with a predictable God?

A predictable God brooks no uncertainty. Everything has been settled once and for all. His subjects know when, where and how he will act every time. God has set up a strict equation between human action and divine reward or punishment. A good deed always gets the same merit, no matter who performs it, or under what circumstances. The same certainty applies to sin. A sinful act always merits the same punishment.

Spiritual life is easy. Study the past and learn the pattern. Choose only the deeds that really count. Say the prayers that stack up. What was worth the most points yesterday will be just as valuable today. No need to waste all day waiting for God to reveal his will. Be ready, though, when you know he is scheduled to speak or to appear. The saint is not the person with the most fervor, but the one with the best memory.

Life with this God is judged by production. And that is as it should be. Everyone knows the rules, everyone knows the point system. A person can be just as holy or mediocre or sinful as he wishes. It is easy to judge your own goodness or sinfulness; better than that, it is easy to judge the progress of others. With a predictable God, one can be suspicious of anything new. What has not already been done or said is obviously not of God. The saintly life is very methodical and repetitious. The unspiritual would say it is dull. But it is safe. God is shackled by his own rules, whether he realizes it or not, and man is in control.

This caricature of spirituality is recognizable as the kind of religious observance Jesus consistently repudiated. The mistake of the Pharisees was to try to squeeze God into a box, bound up in a set of rules for every occasion.

Yahweh our God is not like this at all, though we often treat him as if he were the stiff, colorless deity described above. But he is an unpredictable God, creative and colorful. With our God there is only one certainty: he loves us. We don't know what he will do next, where he will touch us or what he will call us to do, but we know that whatever comes will be another manifestation of that love. The only way to be at peace with this kind of God is to cast yourself into his arms. The New Testament calls this response faith, the "obedience of faith" (Rm 1:5). It is the one sure requirement for a happy life with Yahweh, the father of Jesus and our father.

There is no way to make points with this God by the performance of certain works. No particular action in itself is ever guaranteed to please him; but everything pleases him if it is done in love and with faith surrender. The secret is to live as a child, without pretense or conniving. The good news is the source of our joy and peace, bringing an end to anxiety and fear. We are not doomed to production. As children, we can rely totally on our Father, and in so acting we will be doing everything he asks of us. We will not be judged on the basis of talent or training, on how we speak and influence others, on our popularity, but on how completely we accept the Father's love and radiate it in our life.

Life with this loving God will reflect what Paul calls "the fruit of the spirit": love, joy, peace, patience, kindness, generosity, faith, mildness, self-control (Gal 5:22-23). Christians are joyful, grateful and optimistic. Nothing can separate us from the love of Christ (Rm 8:35-39). The Christian's chief prayer is thanksgiving, Eucharist. There is no need to slash ourselves with knives to get God's attention, like the prophets of Baal (1 K 18:25-29). Our God is always awake, always near and listening. He is Immanuel (Is 7:14; Mt 1:23). We need only open our-selves to him in spirit and truth.

Like a Little Child

In the world of the unpredictable God, every moment is a precious gift, every person a revelation, every place a temple. God may appear anywhere, anytime, in any disguise. And so his child lives the present moment as if it were forever, treating every person reverently as the latest revelation of Yahweh. The believer knows that with a God so personally involved in history there are no mere coincidences. Even the most unforeseen happening is somehow a saving event, an expression of divine love. The Christian must have a sense of wonder to be ready at any moment for the surprise of his life: grace, truth, beauty, suffering, salvation.

The child of the unpredictable God is a free person. He does not have to depend on opinion or precedent. He can take risks in serving, daring, like Jesus, like Peter and Paul, to spread the kingdom in new ways. Our God does not condemn errors of judgment, only sin. The courageous in the kingdom will risk, and they will make mistakes. But they will be nearer the mind of Christ than disciples who play it safe out of fear. "Faith," says Newman, "means that we have the heart to dare something."

The Christian's imitation of Christ is not the mimicry of a particular set of actions. My life may not look like the life of Jesus of Nazareth, because I will not live in Nazareth or Capernaum, or die in Jerusalem. But my life will be like his if my heart is like his, if I am willing to lay down my life for others, and do everything the Father asks. I cannot do simply what others do, even the saints, because the Father may have a different plan for my life. I can only respond day by day as his word to me becomes audible. With God ever present with us on our pilgrimage, we need know only the next step, not the complete travel schedule or even the destination. Chesterton called Christians the people who "go gaily in the dark."

Confidence in a loving Father gives the Christian a sense of humor in regard to his own weakness and failings and toward the embarrassing situations that confront him in this world. It relieves him of the need to cover up; he can lay aside the masks and disguises and be himself. Honesty is the only policy. He can be a fool for Christ's sake, able to dance when no one else hears the music.

The child of the loving, unpredictable God is patient of people's weakness and sensitive to their cries of pain. He is not anxious about others, forcing them to comply to a set of rules "for their own good"; nor does he consider their happiness or success or friendship with God a threat to his own. The Christian shares whatever goods he has with others, knowing that a provident Father will care for him as he does for the lilies of the field and the birds of the sky. Anyway, too much baggage would make it difficult for him to move on; and he must always be sandaled and ready to heed the call, like Abraham of whom Gregory of Nyssa commented: "Abraham left home without knowing which way he was going, a good sign he was going the right way."

Such confidence may seem simplistic and, taken wrongly, could lead to complacency and quietism. Why do anything at all if God does everything? The gospel does not answer, except to preserve the paradox. The Father knows what we need before we ask, and wants to give us the kingdom, but we must still do our part in prayer and work (Mt 6:1-34). We are responsible for the progress of the Church and her mission, but as instruments of God. It is not our plan we are executing, but his.

Because of the nature of the God who speaks his word to us, our response to the word can never be settled beforehand. It has to be listened to and acted on anew every day. We can act on it with absolute confidence because of the faithful love of the Father whose word is always an act of love.

READING SUGGESTIONS

Boylan, Eugene. *This Tremendous Lover*. Westminster, Md.: Newman Press, 1948.

De Sales, St. Francis. *On the Love of God*. Garden City, N. Y.: Image Books, 1963.

Farrell, Edward J.: *The Father is Very Fond of Me*. Denville, N. J.: Dimension Books, 1975.

Van Breemen, Peter G. *As Bread That is Broken*. Denville, N. J.: Dimension Books, 1974.

CHAPTER FOUR

THE GREAT WORD: RESURRECTION

Some of St. Paul's writing is so deep and complex that single passages produce volumes of commentary, but he could be direct and blunt when he wanted to. "If anyone preaches a gospel to you other than the one you received, let a curse be upon him!" (Gal 1:9). The Galatian Judaizers were chopping at the roots of Christianity, and Paul's anger seems to scorch the pages. But Paul did not have to be hot to be clear. To convince the Corinthians of the centrality of the resurrection, he said just as bluntly: "If Christ was not raised, your faith is worthless. You are still in your sins, and those who have fallen asleep in Christ are the deadest of the dead" (1 Cor 15:17-18).

Resurrection is one of those priceless mysteries that has had to suffer the highest compliments for the wrong reasons. We think of ourselves as saved by the death of Jesus, with the resurrection as a fantastic miracle provided to prove that the death was really effective and Jesus is really God. But Paul says that isn't enough. If Christ was not raised, your faith is worthless. Nothing happened. To see the resurrection as only a miracle after the fact of redemption is to sell it short. We are saved by death and resurrection, the emphasis falling on resurrection.

The Paschal Mystery

People are puzzled when they turn to the introduction of their New American Bible and read: "Jesus' death, his resurrection, his ascension and the communication of the Spirit are actually *one* event. It all happened at the very moment of Jesus' death." This seems equivalent to saying that our belief in the different salvation mysteries of Easter, Ascension and Pentecost is naive imagining. But how does this square with the biblical passages which mention three days between death and resurrection, forty days till ascension, and fifty days till the pentecostal coming of the Holy Spirit? Did the author of the introduction read the book?

The statement quoted here, unfamiliar though its message be, is not double-talk. Vatican Council II introduced us to the idea of considering Christ's "blessed passion, resurrection from the dead, and glorious ascension" as the single "paschal mystery" (*Sacrosanctum Concilium*, no. 5). This way of speaking hinges on the fact that from God the Father's eternal point of view, the whole work of salvation in Christ, from incarnation to pentecost, is a single all-sufficient act. But ours is not the long-range overview of eternity, and we know salvation as worked out in successive events in time. We can distinguish the several parts of the one saving act of Christ as it appeared in history: his birth, his ministry of teaching and healing, his death, resurrection, ascension and sending of the Spirit.

Moses led the people of Israel in the original paschal journey from slavery to freedom. Jesus passed from death to life through his passion and resurrection, making it possible for us to follow him to freedom. The Exodus/Passover was the central event of the Old Testament, God's saving word to the people; in a very real sense all the writings of the Old Testament are a meditation on the meaning

of the Exodus. The new Exodus/Passover in Jesus Christ
reveals what the Exodus of Moses was really pointing to:
it is the Great Word of both testaments, and the New
Testament writings are a meditation on its meaning.

Two Kinds of Resurrection

We should be clear about which of the two kinds of
resurrection mentioned in the Gospels is the basis of our
faith. Three people were raised from the dead by Jesus:
the daughter of Jairus, the son of the widow of Naim,
and Lazarus. They were brought back to life, restored to
the earthly conditions they had known before. But they
were doomed to die later on; the victory was incomplete.
This "resurrection" was not a permanent condition. Death
remained waiting in the wings.

The resurrection of Jesus is in a completely different
order. He was not "brought back to life," but broke
through by divine power to a new and permanent form
of life. "Christ having been raised from the dead will
never die again. . . . . His life now is life with God" (Rm
6:8,10). The resurrection of Jesus is a new achievement,
a "new creation" (2 Cor 5:17), something unforeseen
and unknown before. Jesus did not return to earthly life
only to die again; he entered, in his body, a new sphere
of life beyond death.

The idea of bodily resurrection has caused many problems, most of them based on bad information. What
about people who are cremated, or people with ampu-
tated limbs? Will I still be fat in heaven? What happened to the blood Jesus shed on the way to Calvary? The
accounts about Jesus' risen body reveal a tension between two qualities which could otherwise be contra-
dictory: his body is the same, but it has changed. He still
eats fish with the apostles, but he can now go through
closed doors. He still has the wounds of the cross (as

Thomas could tell you), but some of his closest friends (Magdalene, for instance) don't recognize him. What does this mean? It means that the risen Jesus is the same Jesus in the same body, but his body has been glorified. It is transformed. Our faith looks forward to a resurrection like that at the end of time. We will be the same persons in our same bodies, but our bodies will be transformed. "He will give a new form to this lowly body of ours and remake it according to the pattern of his glorified body" (Ph 3:21).

The only serious New Testament effort to explain what the resurrection body will be like is in Chapter 15 of Paul's First Letter to the Corinthians. This was a troublesome issue among Paul's Corinthian converts, with their Platonic notion of the inferiority of the body and its inability to enter the world of "reality." Paul was speaking of our resurrection on the last day, but what he says about our risen body is based on what happened to Jesus. The best he can do with this "nonsensical question" (v. 36) is to answer in metaphor. He compares the present physical body to a seed, the resurrection body to its fruit. "When you sow, you do not sow the fullblown plant, but a kernel of wheat or some other grain. God gives body to it as he pleases—to each seed its own fruition. . . . So it is with the resurrection of the dead. What is sown in the earth is subject to decay, what rises is incorruptible. Weakness is sown, strength rises up. A natural body is put down and a spiritual body comes up" (vv. 37-38, 42-44). Paul doesn't really tell us anything specific, just that you can't imagine by looking at the present body what the resurrection body will be like any more than you can form a mental picture of a flower by looking at its seed. But the transformation will be worth waiting for.

Old Testament Hopes

Up to now, we have tried to understand what happened to Jesus in the resurrection and what will happen to us at the Second Coming. But something already happened to us and all men when Jesus rose. To understand this, we must familiarize ourselves with the expectations of the Old Testament about the redemption to come. The history of the Hebrew people is a classic saga of ups and downs (or better, downs and ups). God formed them into a nation, to begin with, by bringing them out of slavery. Their gratitude was brief: they quickly broke the covenant he had made with them. Time and again they failed him, turning to the man-made gods of their neighbors, gods who would condone their greed, immorality, dishonesty. But just as often as they fell, they rose up again. They knew themselves to be people of The Promise, and whenever they forgot it, the prophets were there to remind them and call them back. The remarkable thing—it is the mark of God's love—is that they were able to revive so many times. The story is in cycles of sin and repentance, slavery and freedom, exile and return.

The curse of sin and the tendency to discouragement were always there, and many fell away. But a faithful core remembered the promise and kept it alive; someday, they knew, the pattern of downs and ups would come to an end in a final up. Their view of history was optimistic: justice would overcome sin, freedom slavery, and life death. The Israelites looked forward to the day when the bonds would be broken for the last time, when the shackles of sin would fall away, when the old covenant with its external demands would give way to a new internal covenant.

The great Day of the Lord was to usher in fulfillment of the promise and final victory for the faithful Israelites. It was to be the ultimate regeneration: "No longer shall your sun go down, or your moon withdraw, for the Lord will be your light forever, and the days of your mourning shall be at an end" (Is 60:20). The special gift of this eschatological or end time was to be the spirit of the Lord: "I will pour my spirit on all mankind. Your sons and daughters shall prophesy, your old men shall dream dreams, and your young men shall see visions" (Jl 3:1-2).

By "spirit of the Lord," the Old Testament people did not mean the Third Person of the Trinity in the full Christian sense. The Trinity was not yet revealed. The spirit of the Lord meant a special manifestation of God's power and presence. The great leaders of Israel—Moses, Samuel, David—had received a special gift of the spirit of the Lord, as had the prophets. In the Day of the Lord, said the prophets, the spirit of the Lord will not be rationed to a select number of God's people, but will be poured out in abundance on all. "I shall give you a new heart, and put a new spirit in you: I shall remove the heart of stone from your bodies and give you a heart of flesh instead. I shall put my spirit in you" (Ezk 36:26-27). The power of this spirit to regenerate a sinful, hopeless, lifeless people is portrayed in the famous "Dem Bones" vision of Ezekiel 37. In connection with this day of victory, the Hebrews expected a salvation figure called the "Anointed One" (in Hebrew "Messiah," in Greek "Christ"). He would be the greatest prophet and leader of all, surpassing even Moses and David. He would be anointed by the spirit of the Lord more thoroughly than ever before. "The spirit of the Lord shall rest upon him; a spirit of wisdom and of understanding, a spirit of counsel and of strength, a spirit of knowledge and of fear of the Lord" (Is 11:2).

Jesus, the Spirit-bearer

The New Testament writers see all these foreshadow-

ings fulfilled in a surpassing way in Jesus Christ. Notice
the many references to the spirit of the Lord (now the
"Holy Spirit") right from the beginning of the Gospels.
It is especially noticeable in Luke. "The angel answered
Mary: 'The Holy Spirit will come upon you and the
power of the Most High will overshadow you'" (Lk
1:35). The Holy Spirit inspires Zechariah and Elizabeth
to recognize the significance of Jesus' birth (Lk 1:41-
42, 67-79). The baptism of Jesus, the scene of the inaug-
uration of his public ministry, is a special occasion of
the Spirit's coming on him. When Jesus gives his keynote
sermon in the Nazareth synagogue, his text is from Isaiah, "The spirit of the Lord is upon me; therefore he
has anointed me" (Lk 4:18).

Jesus is "full of the Holy Spirit" (Lk 4:1), the authentic spirit-bearing messenger of God. But even he
could not fulfill the messianic hope of a universal outpouring of the Spirit during his time of public ministry.
As a consequence of the self-emptying involved in God's
plan of incarnation (Ph 2:5-11), the Spirit did not yet
penetrate Christ's humanity completely. In becoming
man, the Son of God freely accepted the limitations of
humanity. He was thoroughly human, with every human
weakness we experience, except for sin (Heb 4:15). He
did bring healing and the presence of the Spirit to individuals, but he could not give the Spirit universally while
he was still an "earthly body." His humanity had to be
glorified before it would be fully penetrated by the Holy
Spirit and opened out with saving grace for all men.
John mentions this limitation when Jesus speaks of the
living water he will give: "Here he was referring to the
Spirit whom those that came to believe in him were to
receive. There was, of course, no Spirit as yet, since
Jesus had not yet been glorified" (Jn 7:37-39).

The breakthrough came in Jesus' resurrection. This
was crucial to our redemption. Eternal life is in us by

the working of the Holy Spirit; it is the presence of the Spirit in us. Without this Holy Spirit, there would be no living the life of Christ, no sacraments, no Church. We would be earthbound, unable to be transformed bodily for life in heaven. "Flesh and blood cannot inherit the kingdom of God; no more can corruption inherit incorruption" (1 Cor 15:50).

It was through the resurrection that Jesus became glorified in his body and capable of pouring out the Holy Spirit everywhere and forever. He broke through to new unending life, "life for God" (Rm 6:10). St. Paul sees in the resurrection the beginning of a new world order, a "new creation" (2 Cor 5:17). In the Gospels of Matthew and Mark, the severing with the past is symbolized by the splitting of the Temple veil (Mt 27:51; Mk 15:38). The earth itself responds in storm clouds, darkness, and earthquake. In the resurrection, Christ's body is flooded with the blinding light of God's glory, an event foreshadowed by the Transfiguration. His humanity now becomes the eternal instrument of salvation. Christ is so filled with life that he will pour it forth forever. Early Christian preachers could speak of the resurrection as the "real" birth of Christ as savior (Ac 13:33; Rm 1:4).

The Birth of the Church

This outpouring of the Spirit inaugurates Christian salvation and founds the Church. At pentecost, weak, timid men are transformed into the Church of Christ. The apostles are spirit-filled and able to speak boldly about the wonderful works of God. Far from being hesitant now, they "cannot help but proclaim what we have heard and seen" (Ac 4:20). Peter interprets the strange happenings of pentecost by declaring the fulfillment of the Joel prophecy: "It shall come to pass in the last days, says God, that I will pour out a portion of my spirit on all mankind" (Ac 2:17). And he summarizes resurrection, ascension and pentecost in a single verse: "Exalted at God's right hand, he first received the promised Holy Spirit from the Father, then poured this Spirit out on us" (Ac 2:33).

The salvation sequence is one continuous event flowing from resurrection. The Gospels of Luke and John show ascension and pentecost happening on Easter day (Lk 24:50-51; Jn 20:22). But St. Luke has been a cause of confusion because he is also the writer who, in the Acts of the Apostles, describes a forty-day interval till ascension and a fifty-day interval till pentecost. He is treating the same events from different points of view. Luke knows that the resurrection mystery in Christ is all-inclusive, that complete salvation was won at Easter. But he also knows that the early Christian community was not immediately aware of the implications of Christ's victory. In Acts, Luke pictures the infant Church's experience of the saving event. Christ "showed himself alive to them after his Passion by many demonstrations" (Ac 1:3), but these were not last-minute goodbyes before he returned to his Father. Jesus was already glorified with the Father since the resurrection; all these appearances were from heaven. But on the fortieth day, says Luke, the apostles experienced the definitive leave-taking of Christ in his human form; he would still be with them but bodily appearances would no longer be needed to convince them of his resurrection.

Acts 2 portrays in the pentecost story the infant community's later realization of what had taken place at Easter: the outpouring of the Holy Spirit to be the source of life for Jesus' followers. After the fear and wonder and misunderstanding of the death and resurrection, the Christians experienced in a vivid manner the coming of the unifying, life-giving Spirit. It is this "birthday of the Church" that we commemorate each year in the celebration of pentecost, praying that a new out-pouring of the Holy Spirit will again enliven faith, awaken courage, and deepen joy.

Resurrection Today

The resurrection of Jesus happened historically, but it does not belong to the past. As the act of redemption of the God-man, the resurrection shares in divine eternity and is always present and effective. Humanity was introduced to a kind of living unknown before. Christian life is lived in the permanent moment of the resurrection. The New Testament is full of the excitement this realization brings: "Praised be the God and Father of our Lord Jesus Christ, he who in his great mercy gave us new birth; a birth unto hope which draws its life from the resurrection of Jesus Christ from the dead, a birth to an imperishable inheritance" (1 P 1:3-4); "Our hope is no delusion, because the love of God has been poured into our hearts by the Holy Spirit who has been given to us" (Rm 5:5).

As the truth of Jesus' resurrection began to sink into the apostles and disciples, they were puzzled why everything seemed to be just as it had been before. On Easter morning the Romans were still in control of the country and the Jews were still hostile to Jesus and his followers. People still had to eat and drink and work and sleep. It was hard to grasp a new age in which everything was the same as before. It was only gradually that they comprehended what had happened. For a while they still expected the end to come quickly. Even twenty years later some Thessalonians had to be chided for stopping work in expectation of Christ's immediate return.

These Christians were not completely wrong; in fact, they drew the proper conclusion in thinking that the resurrection marked the end of the world. But the mystery was more profound than they had at first perceived.

The resurrection of Jesus is the final word of God to man in history. In the resurrection, the last day has arrived, the end of the world has broken into history. The shackles of sin are broken, the gates of heaven are open. There is only the single moment of resurrection.

From Glory to Glory

Sin and redemption continue to fight a battle in each of us. We still have to accept the victory personally. Like Paul, we experience the "law of sin" in ourselves, making us do what in our heart of hearts we do not want to do (Rm 7:15-23). But we are confident that the transformation is going on in the present, because the Holy Spirit, the principle of resurrection, dwells in us (Rm 8:11). He is the seal of present salvation and the pledge of future blessedness (2 Cor 1:21-22). If the trappings could fall away, we would be able to see the process of glorification working in our mortal bodies even now. "All of us, gazing on the Lord's glory with unveiled faces, are being transformed from glory to glory into his very image by the Lord who is the Spirit" (2 Cor 3:18).

The presence of this transforming Spirit in our members gives us the responsibility of apostles: to witness to resurrection (Ac 1:22). We are repositories of Christ's life-giving energy, "children of resurrection" (Lk 20: 36). Like Christ we are filled with the resurrection life, and have to pour it out. We do this primarily by being signs of life in a world of death, spreading optimism, joy, peace, justice, truth. We take it as our mission to heal wounds, to make people feel good about themselves, accepted and loved. "What we have seen and heard we proclaim to you that you may share life with us" (1 Jn 1:3). It is the Spirit who transforms us and the Spirit within us who transforms those who meet us. We cannot change or save people, but the Spirit in us can work this miracle within the context that our love provides.

Through us the risen Lord continues to roll away stones from tombs and lead people from death to life. "Offer yourselves to God as men who have come back from the dead to life, and your bodies to God as weapons for justice" (Rm 6:13).

READING SUGGESTIONS

Collins, T. P. *The Risen Christ in the Fathers of the Church*. Glen Rock, N. J.: Paulist Press, 1967.

Durrwell, F. X. *The Resurrection*. New York: Sheed and Ward, 1960.

Guardini, Romano. *The Lord*. Chicago: Regnery, 1954.

Haughton, Rosemary. *The Transformation of Man*. Springfield, Ill.: Templegate, 1967.

CHAPTER FIVE

THE DEATH THAT LEADS TO LIFE

The early Christian preachers found many ways to phrase the message of divine salvation in Jesus Christ, but the kernel of their proclamation was always the paschal mystery: "You put to death the Author of life; but God raised him from the dead and we are his witnesses" (Ac 3:15); "He died for our sins and rose for our justification" (Rm 4:25). In the preceding chapter some attention was devoted to the fact that our redemption involves a series of events: death, resurrection, ascension, pentecost. We could even add to both ends of the series and say that the mystery includes Jesus' whole life and the Parousia or Second Coming, which is simply the full unfolding of the resurrection.

The parts of this single mystery do follow one another in order, though. Each member of the series flows from another. Resurrection leads directly to ascension-glorification, which necessarily involves the outpouring of the Holy Spirit, and so on. This interconnection of aspects of the paschal mystery explains why this chapter on the death of Jesus follows the chapter on the resurrection, instead of preceding it in the normal order. The resurrection of Jesus flows directly from his death. Before attempting to understand his death it was helpful to investigate the goal and climax of that death.

Resurrection does not issue from just any kind of

death, but from the kind of death that Jesus died. St. Paul alludes to this when he bases his hope of resurrection on the possibility of being "formed into the pattern of his death" (Ph 3:10-11), and says, "If we have been united with him through likeness to his death, so shall we be through a like resurrection" (Rm 6:5). The important question for us is: What kind of death is this? What is the pattern of Jesus' death, the pattern that leads to resurrection?

The Death of Jesus

First of all, this special kind of death is not merely physical. In fact, it isn't even necessary to die physically in order to do the kind of dying that leads to the transformation of resurrection. This stands out in another statement of St. Paul: "Not all of us shall fall asleep, but all of us are to be changed—in an instant, in the twinkling of an eye, at the sound of the last trumpet. The trumpet will sound and the dead will be raised incorruptible, and we shall be changed" (1 Cor 15:51-52). When he wrote this, Paul was still expecting to be alive when Christ came back. He did not think physical death a prerequisite to resurrection. We do not have to die in order to rise from the dead—to be "changed," or glorified, as Jesus was.

We know well that Jesus died by crucifixion in the midst of immense suffering. This has caused many people to confuse the outer trappings with the meaning of his death. It was not the kind or amount of pain that made his dying redemptive. "We were reconciled to God by the death of his Son because of its special qualities," wrote St. Thomas Aquinas. "It was not Christ's death simply as death which so pleased the Father that it reconciled men to him. God does not rejoice in the death of the living. It was rather the fact that it proceeded from the will of Christ; for Christ willed to die out of obedience to the Father and out of love for men" (*Commentary on Romans*, 5:10). We are saved because Jesus gave himself completely in love and obedience. It is that kind of death, and only that kind of death in God's plan, that is redemptive and leads to resurrection. To "die like Jesus" is to give ourselves to life in obedient love.

For the sake of clarity it should be pointed out that the New Testament speaks of three different kinds of death, relying on the context to bring out the meaning. The first and most important kind of death is the redemptive act of Christ we have been considering, the loving gift of self in response to the Father's will. There is also death in its standard meaning of end of physical life. The third meaning of death is the sinful state that drags people down, separating them from God. It is attachment to "the world" or "the flesh," or simply "sin," which without conversion and forgiveness becomes eternal death: "To set the mind on the flesh is death" (Rm 8:6); "Passion gives birth to sin, and when sin reaches maturity it begets death" (Jm 1:15).

By meeting this sinful death head-on, by accepting willingly the self-emptying that is the curse of death, Jesus "robbed death of its power" (2 Tm 1:10). He reversed the sinful attitude of disobedience and sinful pride that had condemned man in a state of sin. Jesus made self-emptying the way to fulfillment, death the way of life. The whole movement of redemption through this death into resurrection is captured masterfully in the early hymn recorded by Paul in his letter to the Philippians. The poem seems to follow the steps of the catechumen down into the baptismal font, where he is plunged into the death-resurrection of Jesus and climbs out the other side living a new life.

> Your attitude must be that of Christ.
> Though he was in the form of God,
>   he did not deem equality with God

something to be grasped at.
Rather, he emptied himself
    and took the form of a slave,
    being born in the likeness of men.
He was known to be of human estate,
    and it was thus that he humbled himself,
    obediently accepting even death,
    death on a cross!
Because of this,
    God highly exalted him
    and bestowed on him the name
    above every other name,
So that at Jesus' name
    every knee must bend
    in the heavens, on the earth,
    and under the earth,
    and every tongue proclaim
    to the glory of God the Father:
    Jesus Christ is Lord! (Ph 2:5-11).

The key to the Christian mystery lies at the center of this poem, at the bottom of the steps. Jesus' self-giving to the point of death seems a loss, a waste, but because of this, he is raised on high. Not in spite of but because of the way he died, Jesus was glorified. "Jesus is crowned with glory and honor because he suffered death: Jesus, who was made for a little while lower than the angels, that through God's gracious will he might taste death for the sake of all men" (Heb 2:9).

The Pattern of Salvation

As our leader Jesus goes before, cutting the path ahead of us. His way must be our way, through death to life. This is established as the permanent pattern of Christian salvation: resurrection flows from the kind of death Jesus died. "If any man would come after me, let him deny himself and take up his cross and follow me" (Mk 8:34). The promise is anything but romantic. Most of us find ourselves in the shoes of James and John, trying to find a shortcut into the kingdom.

" 'Teacher,' they said, 'we want you to grant our request. . . . See to it that we sit, one at your right and the other at your left, when you come into your glory.' " Jesus responded by asking them a loaded question: " 'Can you drink the cup I shall drink or be baptized in the same bath of pain as I?' 'We can,' they replied." The apostles did not perceive that the full meaning of "drinking the cup" is suffering and death with Jesus. They seized what sounded like an easy agreement. Jesus took them at their word. "From the cup I drink of you shall drink" (Mk 10:35-45).

From the beginning of our life with Jesus we have been "baptized into his death" (Rm 6:3). Baptism is the beginning of dying to self by living for others in obedience to the Father. This dying is another word for love. "That we have passed from death to life we know because we love the brothers. The man who does not love is among the living dead. . . . The way we came to understand love was that he laid down his life for us; we too must lay down our lives for our brothers" (1 Jn 3:14-16). As we move relentlessly toward physical death, hopefully this real death is taking place in us. Our goal is to arrive at the moment of physical self-emptying with our interior self-emptying complete: physical death and the death of Christ in us coinciding in victory over sinful death. Our physical death will then be, as it is in the saints and was supremely in the case of Jesus, the sacrament of our interior dying.

The Church provides us with daily reminders of our vocation to share the death of Jesus. The chief of these is the Cup of the Eucharist. When the cup is raised and the priest says, "Take this, all of you, and drink from it," his invitation is not limited to the particular vessel he is raising. Whether one partakes from that particular cup or not, each worshiper must renew his covenant by accepting the dying of Jesus symbolized in the sacred cup. Each use of holy water with the sign of the Cross should remind us of the baptism that plunged us into the death of Jesus.

The dying to self is helped positively by the asceticism that tradition has called very accurately "mortification"—putting to death. We have to wage a campaign against the forces that would enslave us. Paul speaks of being crucified to the world (Gal 6:14); "Those who belong to Christ Jesus have crucified their flesh with its passions and desires" (Gal 5:24). Never is Christian mortification to be an exercise in morbid piety. It is following Jesus to Calvary to learn how to love.

Dying and Rising

Resurrection comes through dying with Jesus. We can still be mistaken about the full significance of this mystery by considering Christian death and resurrection only consecutively: die now, rise later. The truth is richer than that. We die and rise now. If we are sharing the death of Jesus now, we are also being transformed now. Death and life grow together day by day in the Christian life. "Continually we carry about in our bodies the dying of Jesus, so that in our bodies the life of Jesus may also be revealed. While we live we are constantly being delivered to death for Jesus' sake, so that the life of Jesus may be revealed in our mortal flesh" (2 Cor 4:11-12). Where there is the death of Jesus there is resurrection; where there is no self-giving love, though, there can be no risen life. Resurrection life and joy cannot be faked. If not backed up by love, it has a tinny sound, like a noisy gong or a clanging cymbal (1 Cor 13:1). We cannot express the resurrection of Jesus unless we have begun to share the dying which brings it about. But where there is love, no suffering can diminish the resonance of Christian joy. "We do not lose heart, because our inner being is renewed each day even though our body is being destroyed at the same time" (2 Cor 4:16).

The Synoptic Gospels present the mission of Jesus in stages, beginning in Galilee and ending in Jerusalem. At a certain moment in his ministry Jesus knew that it was time to set in motion the events that would cost him his last drop of blood. "He set his face to go to Jerusalem" (Lk 9:51). Jesus realized that he was heading for physical destruction. All that is natural in a human being rebels against this final defeat, this disintegration. But Jesus went forward to do his Father's will in absolute trust, already dying the redemptive death. Jerusalem is not to be only the scene of his death. It is the place of resurrection. And so as Jesus nears Jerusalem, he is approaching death and resurrection with the same steps. The closer he comes to victory, the nearer is he to defeat, the more acute is the pain. The crisis of suffering culminates in the Garden and on the cross.

This journey of Jesus to Jerusalem is a symbol of our own journey. As we progress toward the fullness of resurrection, we know more and more what the death entails. As our joy in resurrection intensifies, so does the acuteness of our pain. We are more aware of the beauty and goodness of God, but also more sensitive to our own sinfulness and the weakness of others. We see injustice and dishonesty, seeds of hatred and war, that our eyes could not perceive before. And so, as we near the holy city, the dying and the rising in our lives grow more intense together. We can suffer more deeply than ever, we can rejoice as never before.

This entwining of death and life preserves us from extremes of sadness and giddiness in our spiritual life. Spirituality has not always kept this balance. Medieval piety was preoccupied with the death of Jesus. As time went on, this led to aberrations which drained the joy from Christ's victory. Interest in the details of Christ's agony, reflected in art and spiritual exercises of the day, became morbid and pessimistic. Suffering and sadness became ultimate values. A principle of spirituality arose: what is harder is better, what is enjoyable is suspect.

This gloomy Christianity felt a severe reaction with the recovery of resurrection theology in this country, especially in the wake of Vatican II. But as is often the case, the reaction led to aberrations itself. In some circles Christian spirituality became bubbly and flighty. Its principle then became: whatever is enjoyable is good, whatever hurts is bad. It was a baptism of the "noble savage" philosophy, involving a practical denial of man's sinfulness and need of redemption. The full mystery of Christian spirituality is the combination of death and resurrection. Neither the harder nor the easier way is always better; the holy way is response to the current call of the Lord.

Witnesses of Resurrection

Though our life blends death and resurrection, it is only resurrection that the world must see. We are witnesses of resurrection. Our vibrant joy is a public gift for the whole world. Our dying is the underside of this resurrection; it must be kept secret. Our inner death, our suffering, our mortification, this must remain hidden. We do not flaunt it, because it has to remain in the darkness of the earth to come to life. "I tell you solemnly, unless the grain of wheat falls to the earth and dies, it remains just a grain of wheat. But if it dies, it produces much fruit" (Jn 12:24). If our dying is brought into the air and sunlight, it begins to decay and smell. It must remain hidden in the earth of our bodies, like a seed, if it is to germinate and flower in resurrection.

This is the most difficult challenge in dying with Christ. We cannot bear to keep it secret. How much we want others to know the pain we are experiencing. We need to have the whole world aware of the mistreatment we are getting, our hard work, our physical aches and pains, our patient endurance. We like to practice religion before men. But Jesus warned: "If you do these things publicly you will not have any reward from your Father in heaven" (Mt 6:1). Bernanos' country priest saw another effect: "When our suffering has been dragged from one pity to another, as from one mouth to another, we can no longer respect or love it, I feel." The Christian must be transparently honest and real, but there is one mask he must wear: it is the Christian mask of resurrection over death.

This is not to deny the place of confession, spiritual direction and counseling in our spiritual journey. We need to share our interior life with someone. We cannot keep the pain of Christian dying completely locked inside. But it is not to be broadcast or flaunted. One or two of our closest friends and spiritual guides are enough to help make sense of our personal death and resurrection and accept it in faith and joy. Such friends are able to detect illusion and give a reliable assessment of strength and weakness, progress and failure.

In bearing witness to resurrection, we are proclaiming the redemptive death of Christ. But our nature prefers to bear witness to another kind of death, the death of sin. Instead of dying secretly to our own sins, we like to call attention to weakness in others, to expose error, dishonesty, hypocrisy. Our pride makes us want to destroy whatever detracts from our own importance and glory. This surfaces in the need to backbite and gossip, to "murmur," as did the people in the wilderness (Nb 11). We find ourselves rejoicing at the downfall of others when it removes obstacles to our own stardom. We are on the lookout for things to condemn—movements, initiatives, individuals. This is bearing witness to death.

But our vocation is to bear witness to resurrection. The world needs our proclamation of the joy and hope and peace of the kingdom. People see plenty of death in the violence, hatred, dishonesty, greed and passion all around. As witnesses to resurrection we help the world find new ways to express love and justice and peace, drawing attention to people who live like Christ by their self-sacrifice, their fidelity to conscience, their forgiving, their love. We join people who are doing good under all kinds of banners. If we really live this way, the world will know clearly enough about sin. It will be convicted of sin by our living what is good more than by our pointing out what is bad. In a strong light the shadow stands out. We are called to be a light on a mountaintop, not a flashlight in a corner.

The Seed of Christian Dying

The seed of our dying will create in us a resurrection joy in turn creative of life. All of us know people who live like this, persons who take the attention off their own suffering by attending to others, by smiling, by spreading hope. They impress us by their saintliness in the simple consistency of their faith. The fathers and mothers who work too hard and with too little of this world's goods, but with a smile, to raise a family, the sick and handicapped who see the brighter side, the happy searcher who gets the raw end of every deal, the person who helps his tormentors as if the opportunity is a favor to him: these are images of resurrection bringing Christ into our midst.

Occasionally our lives are touched by particularly strong witnesses of the dying of Jesus. In the mid-Sixties our monastery hosted an interracial workshop through Friendship House. It was a time of racial bitterness and violence in the South. A young college graduate from

Little Rock was spending his first year out of school working for voter registration among the blacks of eastern Arkansas. It was dangerous work. We asked him if he had suffered violence in his efforts. He told us quietly about the times he had been beaten with chains, kicked and spit upon. Why don't you fight back, we asked him. "I did at first," he said. "But then I realized that hate must die. If I respond to hate in kind, it bounces off me back into the world. It continues to arch out and harm people. Somewhere this hate has to come to rest. I know now that I must let it die in my body."

Each of us, in large and small ways, must live like this, letting hate die in our bodies. When we do, we cooperate in a transformation greater than the change of water into wine. Sin is turned into grace. It is a kind of transubstantiation. A little dying won't kill you. On the contrary, the suffering accepted in faith and love becomes, by the power of the Holy Spirit in our hearts, the seed of resurrection. "It is in dying that we are born to eternal life" (Prayer of St. Francis). What enters as death returns to the world as life. Love is born of hate.

The climax of our celebration of life through death comes in the Mass. One of the acclamations, quoting Paul (1 Cor 11:26), sums up the mystery: "When we eat this bread and drink this cup we proclaim your death, Lord Jesus, until you come in glory." Death here is not only the event of Calvary two thousand years ago. The love and obedience Jesus poured forth then is still present and living in the eternal moment of resurrection. But the death proclaimed here is not only his, it is ours. We proclaim our death, the death of Jesus in us that is bringing us to life right now. It is the basis of our hope. "I wish to know Christ and the power flowing from his resurrection; likewise to know how to share in his sufferings by being formed into the pattern of his death. Thus do I hope that I may arrive at resurrection from the dead" (Ph 3:10-11).

READING SUGGESTIONS

Ahern, Barnabas. *New Horizons*. Notre Dame: Fides, 1963.

Kazantzakis, Nikos. *The Last Temptation of Christ*. New York: Bantam Books, 1961.

Newman, John Henry. *Apologia Pro Vita Sua*. Garden City, N. Y.: Image Books, 1956.

Taylor, Michael J., ed. *The Mystery of Suffering and Death*. Staten Island: Alba House, 1973.

CHAPTER SIX

THE WORD OF GRACE IN THE CHURCH

In Ignazio Silone's *Bread and Wine,* Don Paolo tries to convince a peasant woman that she does not need to "buy" the blessing of God for her unborn baby. He tells her that grace is free, a gift of God. "There is no such thing as free grace," she responds. The Good News of free salvation is too good for her. She cannot accept God's "word of grace" (Ac 14:3).

Perhaps it is the same for us. Do we really believe that God is the loving Father he claims to be? Can we believe that God offers forgiveness of sin, grace and eternal life free, that we only have to accept his gift in faith?

> All men are now undeservedly justified by the gift of God, through the redemption wrought in Christ Jesus. . . . Now, when a man works, his wages are not regarded as a favor but as his due. But when a man does nothing, yet believes in him who justifies the sinful, his faith is credited as justice" (Rm 3:24; 4:4-5).

In Chapter Three we described the situation of a person who wants to earn grace. Men have a natural desire to earn what they get and get what they earn. A doctrine of free grace is suspicious. Rules are safer and surer. This mentality may be even more pronounced among Americans; it is part of our ethic to be beholden to nobody. It is easier to give gifts than to receive them. We like to brag about making good deals on cars, TVs, services, but we would be reluctant to take the same price breaks if they were offered as gifts. A God who demands a certain number of works, a demonstrable loyalty before bestowing his gifts, is understandable. But our God gives us everything with no strings attached, if we will only accept it in our freedom. "Earning salvation" is true only in metaphor, for the sole block to grace is refusal to accept it. "Love, then, consists in this: not that we have loved God, but that he has loved us and has sent his Son as an offering for our sins" (1 Jn 4: 10).

People who are pessimistic about themselves are pessimistic about the world they live in. If grace is scarce for me, the world is profane, an evil place. God tolerates it as a testing ground for men, but sees nothing good or permanent in the world as such. Thus religion focuses on the God above or beyond and becomes an exercise in the otherworldly. Worship is an escape into the realm of the sacred, a periodical tanking-up of spiritual power for the next few miles amid the dangers of the world. There are subtle ways of succumbing to this false religion. The Church is to be concerned with men's souls, the thinking may go, and spend her time preaching and administering sacraments and teaching people to pray. Priests, brothers and sisters should stay in their sanctuaries and leave the problems of labor and politics and social welfare to men of the world. Religion is one thing, the business of everyday living is another. Vatican II has called this division of life into religious and secular categories "one of the more serious errors of the age" (*Gaudium et Spes*, no. 43).

To believe in the redemptive incarnation of Jesus Christ is to believe that the world is permeated by God's grace. It is a world transformed by resurrection. The world found its focus in the Savior in whom the Father gave himself to man in the most complete way. In his all-embracing will to save men through Christ, the Father made salvation available to men from the beginning of human history (*Lumen Gentium* no. 9). But men are free to reject the gift and the giver through the pride that has ever been the foe of faith.

The Meaning of Grace

The word "grace" has been used liberally in the preceding paragraphs. Before we go any further, the question must be raised: What is grace exactly? Grace is above all the presence of God. It is God himself at home within the believer. To speak in terms familiar to the theme of this book, grace is the seed of God's word working in the heart inspired by faith. It is what the New Testament refers to in speaking of the indwelling of the Trinity. "Anyone who loves me will be true to my word, and my Father will love him; we will come to him and make our dwelling place with him" (Jn 14:23). We are chosen by the Father to share the life of his Son through the Spirit he sends, the "first gift to those who believe" (Fourth Eucharistic Prayer; Jn 13:16). Grace is the love of God "poured out in our hearts through the Holy Spirit who has been given to us" (Rm 5:5).

"Grace" is a predominantly Pauline term in the New Testament. The Greek *charis*, "divine favor," corresponds to the Hebrew *hesed*, the rich Old Testament word for God's covenant love. Nearly every letter of Paul begins by invoking God's grace on the community he is addressing. "Grace and peace to you from God our Father and the Lord Jesus Christ" (1 Cor 1:3). The grace of God is shown in the generous self-sacrifice of Jesus, who "made himself poor though he was rich, so that you might become rich by his poverty" (2 Cor 8:9).

Particular outpourings of this divine favor are called

charismata, charisms. Charisms are gifts to individual
Christians to be used for speech and service (1 Pet 4:10),
for building up the Body of Christ (1 Cor 14:3-5). Paul
lists some of these: apostleship, prophecy, teaching, working miracles, healing, helping, administrating, speaking
in tongues. These gifts of grace make us dispensers of
God's favor, whether by personality or service or special
ministry. "To each person the manifestation of the Spirit
is given for the common good" (1 Cor 12:7).

God's grace is an utterly free gift (Ep 2:8). Paul is
convinced of the futility of trying to gain acceptance
by God through works of the Law. Man is unable to
make himself just, so God justifies man. Grace makes man
acceptable to God in spite of sin, weakness, unworthiness.
"By God's favor I am what I am" (1 Cor 15:10). Grace
is not a reward for good conduct. Rather it rescues the
sinner from hopelessness to enable him to walk faithfully.
Christians do not live holily in order to gain God's favor.
They are enabled to live holily by the grace that has been
bestowed.

Though grace is offered everywhere and continually
by the Father, it is not born into man as a natural consequence of his presence in a graced world. It cannot be
inherited from a believing parent. The gift of grace and
the call to life in God are personal. It is the word of God
calling to authentic human existence. Original sin means
that man cannot of his own power become what he is
meant to be. The sinful man is blind to reality and bound
to unhappiness. He cannot overturn pride and self-cen-
teredness on his own, but needs divine power and presence.
The time comes when, in Christ, God summons each
person to authentic human life—to love, to service, to
honesty, to self-knowledge, to clear vision. No one can
pull himself up to this humanness by his bootstraps. But
by response to grace in faith, a man says yes to the divine
initiative; he accepts the call to become himself, to re-

place his values with the true gospel, to cast out the self-ishness and despair which would otherwise doom him to eternal unhappiness. He accepts the human life of Jesus of Nazareth as the model of his own and the resurrection as the pledge of his own victory.

Grace and Salvation

There is a typical view of salvation which conceives of the Church as the collection of the saved and of the sacraments as the means of access to grace. The thinking goes something like this: Christ came to save mankind from sin. To continue his work he left a Church with the means of salvation for all who would hear his voice through her. Christ's work of salvation continues in the Church, and the Mass and sacraments are the means of distributing the grace he has won on the Cross. The sacraments are the ordinary economy of salvation; one who neglects the sacraments or does not even know about them may achieve heaven by an extraordinary act of divine mercy, but the odds are against him.

This idea of salvation will undoubtedly linger for a long time, but it is on its deathbed, having been dealt a mortal blow by the bishops of Vatican II. Grace is not something for the select few, and salvation is not decided by membership in the Church. The Council's view of salvation is much broader.

> God himself is not far distant from those who in shadows and images seek the unknown, for it is he who gives to all men life and breath and every other gift, and who as Savior wills that all men be saved. Those also can attain to everlasting salvation who through no fault of their own do not know the gospel of Christ or his Church, yet sincerely seek God and, moved by grace, strive by their deeds to do his will as it is known to them through the dictates of con-

science (*Lumen Gentium*, no. 16).

Since Christ died for all men, and since the ultimate vocation of man is in fact one, and divine, we ought to believe that the Holy Spirit in a manner known only to God offers to every man the possibility of being associated with this paschal mystery (*Gaudium et Spes, no.* 22).

The bishops do not speak of a special type of grace available to men who do not know the gospel; the grace of salvation is everywhere the grace of Christ, whether it is recognized as such or not.

The Council Fathers were translating into modern terms the biblical theme of God's universal saving will: "God wants all men to be saved and come to know the truth" (1 Tm 2:4). They had to correct an extreme interpretation of the ancient axiom, "Outside the Church there is no salvation," which proclaimed that only baptized members of the Roman Catholic Church had any chance of reaching heaven. The bishops saw a wider sense of "Church" in this axiom: wherever saving grace is active, Christ is present. This is the way St. Augustine saw it, in a text quoted by Vatican II:

Many who seem to be without are actually within; and many who seem to be within, are really without. . . . . It is certainly clear that when we speak of "within" and "without" with regard to the Church, our consideration must be directed to what is in the heart, not to what is in the body (*Lumen Gentium*, no. 14, n. 2: *Bapt. c. Donat.*, V, 28, 39).

St. Justin Martyr had already spoken in even stronger terms in the second century:

We have been taught that Christ was the First-begotten of God; he is the divine Word in whom the whole human race shares, and those who live according to the light of their knowledge are Christians, even if they are considered as being godless (1 *Apol.*, 46).

St. Thomas explained in terms of scholastic theology the act by which a man can be justified without specific knowledge of Christ or his Church:

> If, when a man begins to deliberate about himself, he directs himself to his due end, he will, by means of grace, receive the remission of original sin (S. *Th.* I-II, q. 89, a. 6).

God can make his saving grace available to people in his own mysterious way, inside or outside his Church. The Church is not meant to be the collection of the saved. This community has another purpose, an irreplaceable purpose, as God's people called together in faith. It is to be the sacrament of the world's salvation.

The Church

Strange as it may seem, there was no full-scale conciliar study of the meaning and purpose of the Church until Vatican II. Earlier Councils took the Church for granted and directed their attention to particular doctrines of the Church, most often to areas of belief under fire. Vatican II based its renewal work on a self-examination of the Church and a re-statement of the Church's role in the world's salvation.

The Council Fathers did not have to begin from scratch. Important theological study of the Church had been going on since the revival of ecclesiology in the nineteenth century by John Adam Mohler, Matthias Scheeben and others. Much of this was summed up in Pope Pius XII's 1943 encyclical, *The Mystical Body of Christ,* with dramatic effects on Catholic life and piety.

The Council wanted to bring this whole development into a wider synthesis. They made sacramentality the key to understanding the Church and her mission. The Church is the "universal sacrament of salvation" (*Lumen Gentium*, no. 48), a "standard lifted high for the nations to see" (*Unitatis Redintegratio,* no. 2).

The Church is the visible manifestation of divine redemption. In her, as in Christ during his earthly ministry, the work of divine salvation finds its visible focus. She is the sign for the world of what life means in its fullness. She is the sacrament of divine forgiveness and reconciliation. The Church with her sacraments, signs of present grace, begins as soon as Christ's visible presence in the world ceases. "What was visible in Christ," said St. Leo, "has now passed over into the sacraments of the Church."

The Church, like each one of her individual sacraments, is a sign of past, present, and future realities. As a commemorative sign, she recalls the saving event of the death and resurrection; as a demonstrative sign, she celebrates the presence of grace now and the divine gift of the present moment; as a prognostic sign, she anticipates the consummation of the kingdom in the parousia. The most important of these roles, as far as contemporary mankind is concerned, is the proclamation of salvation in the present moment. It is far easier to believe that redemption happened in the past or will occur at some point in the rosy future than to believe that it is a present reality in a world of greed, lust and war. As the sacrament of present salvation, the Church lives visibly the life of grace that is being lived in hidden ways throughout the world. She removes the anonymity of God's work in the world.

There is a difference between being the sign and seed of God's saving work in the world (*Lumen Gentium*, no. 9) and being the center around which all of human history revolves. The Church is not the goal of God's redemption; the goal is rather the kingdom of God. The Church is not yet the kingdom, though in the Church the kingdom is at work. Jesus' parables gave insight into the elusive nature of this kingdom. Its beginning is insignificant like a mustard seed, and it grows secretly, acting like yeast in the world. The kingdom is in your midst already, but where it is is not always obvious. The full revelation of the kingdom must await the last day.

Jesus in his life and ministry made men aware of the presence of the kingdom; and he passed on to the Church the mission of being its sign and instrument today. The Church does not point to herself. She is the light of the world only as the reflection of Christ, the light of all nations (*Lumen Gentium*, no. 1). As the servant of God and his people in the world, the Church announces by her life that the kingdom is near; it is growing in our midst.

READING SUGGESTIONS

Vatican Council II. *Constitution on the Church.* (*Lumen Gentium*).

Baum, Gregory. *Man Becoming.* New York: Herder and Herder, 1970.

Fransen, Piet. *Divine Grace and Man.* New York: Desclee, 1962.

McBrien, Richard. *Do We Need the Church?* New York: Harper and Row, 1969.

Chapter Seven

SACRAMENTS:
THE SEVEN WORDS OF THE CHURCH

In a way it's too bad that the ancient Greek word for sacrament, "mystery," was not retained down to our present day. *Mysterion* was replaced by the Latin *sacramentum* early in the Church of the West. Mystery in this sense means God's eternal love made visible, but it also bears a modern nuance of secrecy or uncertainty that might be healthy for present discussion. The seven sacraments have been so expertly tagged and catalogued that it is hard for us to confess that there might be gaps or mistakes in our understanding of them. The documents of Vatican II inspired a new look at the sacraments, particularly through the Constitution on the Church, which described the Church herself as the great sacrament of salvation, and the Constitution on the Liturgy, which mandated ritual renewal for the seven sacraments. We are finding out that our smug definition of the sacraments as "effective signs of grace" has much more "mystery" to it than we have been accustomed to admit.

There are some grounds for the classic Protestant charge that Catholics try to get control of God through the sacraments, tying his hands with his own rope. Sacraments are not viewed this way in the authentic teaching, of course, but a popular notion of sacraments often entails a guaranteed effect. The special grace of each sacrament, it says, can be pinpointed; it is given whenever the ritual is observed. Thus more sacraments always produce more grace. Two Masses are better than one, and three are better than two.

The Sacramentality of Life

Every encounter of man with the divine in history is sacramental. A sacrament, in its widest meaning, is simply the visible sign of a hidden reality. A kiss is sacramental as a sign of love, a doubled fist as a sign of anger, and so forth. In a world of space and time, revelation can be received only in some earthly form. Sacraments are visible, audible, tangible signs of God's work in the world of man: every true sacrament is "grace made visible." All life has this sacramental quality. "There is hardly any proper use of material things which cannot thus be directed toward the sanctification of men and the praise of God" (*Sacrosanctum Concilium*, no. 61). God's word comes to us through our human senses. A sacrament is a visible, audible, tangible word.

The supreme example of sacramentality is the incarnation. Jesus is the Word made flesh. Sacramentality is an important key for understanding the Johannine writings of the New Testament. Jesus is the everlasting love and mercy of the Father in human form, visible, audible, tangible. "This is what we proclaim to you: what was from the beginning, what we have heard, what we have seen with our eyes, what we have looked upon and our hands have touched—we speak of the word of life" (1 Jn 1:1). In meeting the earthly Jesus, the disciples were meeting the Father. "How can you say, 'Show us the Father'?" (Jn 14:9). Jesus lived a thoroughly human life, performing the acts proper to men. His followers experienced him as a human person, not as a disguised God. But in all of Jesus' actions, the redeeming God was at work.

Jesus was the sacrament of God, the visible presence in history of divine mercy.

Compared to the Synoptic writers, John records very few of Jesus' miracles, and then he always refers to them as "signs." They are not only astonishing evidence of Jesus' power—though he is not acting as a superstar—but manifestations of his identity and purpose. The first twelve chapters of John's Gospel are arranged as a Book of Signs: the changing of water into wine (Ch. 2), the healing of the official's son (4), the healing of the paralytic at the pool of Bethesda (5), the multiplication of loaves and the walking on the water (6), the healing of the man born blind (9), the raising of Lazarus (11). There are non-miraculous signs, too: the cleansing of the Temple (2:18-25), the washing of the feet of the Apostles (13:1-20), the crucifixion (8:28). A sign may be miraculous or not, but its purpose is to point to a reality within or beyond itself, in this case to the real identity of Jesus and the significance of his action.

Though the Gospel was composed long after the events it records, the signs Jesus worked are not treated as only past history. John is writing for the community of his time and ours. He wanted to impress upon Christian readers that Jesus is still present and active under the cover of signs in the life of the Church. Jesus' works of salvation are perpetuated in the Church by the Spirit, the principle of new life poured out through Jesus' glorification (Jn 7:37-39).

Through the water of Baptism God begets children to himself (3:5-8), pouring forth on them his Spirit: this Spirit in the believer is the source of eternal life (4: 14). The Word become flesh gives his flesh for the life of the world by the power of the Spirit (6:53-63). By the gift of the Spirit the Church exercises her power to forgive sins in the name of Christ (20:22-23).

John puts his emphasis on Baptism and Eucharist, the

two sacraments most intimately connected with the con-
tinuation of the life of Jesus in the Church. The source
of these two sacraments in the sacrificial death of Jesus
is symbolized dramatically in the Calvary scene: "One
of the soldiers thrust a lance into his side, and immediately
blood and water flowed out" (19:34). The Spirit continues to give witness to Jesus through Baptism and Eucharist, through the water and the blood (1 Jn 5:7-8).

The Primary Sacrament

Risen and glorified, Jesus Christ remains forever the
"primary sacrament" of salvation. It is through him,
in the divine plan, that salvation comes to the whole
world. The believer still encounters the Triune God
through Christ. But now that Christ is glorified, salvation
is visibly manifested in his Church, the body of believers,
and the sacraments of the Church are privileged occasions for the encounter with Christ.

> Thus, for well-disposed members of the faithful,
> the liturgy of the sacraments and sacramentals sanc-
> tifies almost every event in their lives; they are given
> access to the stream of divine grace which flows
> from the paschal mystery of the passion, death, and
> resurrection of Christ, the fountain from which all
> sacraments and sacramentals draw their power (Sacro-
> sanctus Concilium, no. 61).

But every event of history is a sacrament of the
Father's will. God speaks to us from within the course
of our daily lives. Men do not have to escape out of
themselves in ecstasy to contact the divine, but touch
God in the midst of their lives. The full implication of
incarnation is captured in Tertullian's words, "The flesh
is the hinge of salvation." Human persons have always
known this in the depths of their hearts. They have expe-

rienced grace in taking the first step to heal a quarrel, in caring for the family, in sharing a coke with a friend. But all religions develop ritual to express visibly the hidden realities and to intensify human contact with the divine. Primitive man often saw deity in nature, and used symbols and gestures for imitation of the divine activity and insertion into the divine sphere. St. Thomas called these spontaneous attempts to reach God through visible ritual "natural sacraments."

Sacramentality is prerequisite even to human communication. It is only through the body that we can reveal ourselves and our intentions to one another. The way we act, our gestures, our speech—these are signals of what is going on inside. Often external symbols are used to reinforce our actions and words. A gift, for example, focuses a life of love and friendship in a particular moment. Intercourse in marriage sacramentalizes the unity of two in one flesh.

The world evoked by the sacraments of worship is not one of clear lines, of scientific precision, of programmed effects, but a world of "mystery." It is full of symbol and poetry and rite. That is one reason the modern Catholic, a citizen of the scientific age, has been ill at ease with the renewal of the sacraments. There was a time when the sacraments could be taken down, piece by piece and bit by bit, for observation under a microscope; cause and effect were clearly labeled, directions for use were clear. The uncertainty of sacramental poetry is disconcerting to some at first. But for most it is coming to mean discovery of the profound spiritual meaning of the Church's signs of salvation.

Sacraments of Law and Church

Earlier we referred to "natural sacraments" among primitive peoples. The Old Testament community had sacraments, too. Circumcision, temple sacrifice, and the various ritual observances were not empty ceremonies. They were sacramental. Theologians have long noted, for example, a relationship between circumcision and justification. What then is the difference between the sacraments of the Law and the sacraments of the Church?

The explanation can be found in the doctrine behind the badly abused theological concept of *ex opere operato*. This terminology, which has often been interpreted to mean the magical production of grace, simply identifies the sacraments of the Church as precise instances when God's saving will is infallibly expressed. In another way of speaking, it means that the word of God is faithfully proclaimed with a defined meaning and purpose. *Ex opere operato* means that we know by faith that the sacraments are acts of the living Christ with particular redemptive purposes. In the sacrament of Reconciliation, for example, there is no doubt that Christ is acting here and now and that his promised purpose is the forgiveness, reconciliation and healing of the sinner.

We can believe this of the sacraments because we believe the Church to be instituted by Christ as the authentic sacrament of the salvation of the world. She is the focus of God's saving action among men. The difference between the sacraments of the Church and the Old Testament sacraments appears here. The Church is the final and definitive presence of God's salvation in the world. In her, despite the weakness of her members, God assures the world of an eternal covenant. She signals the complete achievement of redemption. With Israel it was different. The old covenant was transitory; its sacraments could never speak definitively of God's saving action or reliably signify the gift of grace.

The seven sacraments of the Church are in a different category from all her other sacramental acts. Through these seven ritual signs the Church expresses her character as sacrament of salvation in a unique way. The whole life of the Church is an effective sign of present grace. Christ is acting constantly in hidden ways that are just as powerful as the seven sacraments. These seven are not isolated occasions of the discharge of grace into the world. But these seven signs are special as the Church's official redemptive acts in the name and power of Christ. The Church does not identify the divine presence in every holy act in the life of her members. In these seven sacraments, though, the Church reveals her identity by highlighting seven important instances of her ministry of Christ's salvation.

The Church uses her teaching authority in a comparable way. The Church does not bear witness with the same authority to every teaching of her ordinary magisterium. The Council spoke of a "hierarchy of truths" (*Unitatis Redintegratio*, no. 11). It is only in rare instances that the Church stands behind a teaching with the whole weight of her identity as teacher in the name of Christ. The Church is always teaching and interpreting the truths of salvation, but it is only on very rare occasions that she puts the whole weight of her authority into a decision and proclaims it infallibly. If this teaching is not true, the Church says at these times, I am not true

In a similar way the Church, guided by the Spirit, has singled out seven of her sacramental acts as unique expressions of her own life. In the seven sacraments the Church puts her own identity as sacrament of salvation on the line, saying in effect if Christ is not present and active in this particular way when these conditions are fulfilled, then I am not true, I am not his Body. There are innumerable sacramental signs in the Church's life, innumerable ritual acts involving Christ's presence and powerful divine effect, but these seven signs are sufficient to express the fullness of the sacramental activity of the Church. The doctrine labeled infallible is no more true than any other faithful teaching, and the sacrament does not add anything to the presence of saving grace that is ever present in the eternal moment of resurrection. But the "sacramentalizing" of the Church's teaching role and of her life as the saving presence of grace in official and authoritative actions makes us more aware of these realities and more open to their effect. The soil is better prepared to receive the seed of the word.

The certainty of divine presence and action in the sacraments has often been confused with the certainty of saving effect, as if one of the seven sacraments always gives grace to a recipient. This is the basis for the charge that *ex opere operato* makes the sacraments magical faucets of grace. But the *effect* of a sacrament is no more assured than the effect of any prayer. The effect of the sacraments, "signs of faith," is dependent on the disposition of the recipient. The seed has life, but it will grow only where there are conditions for growth. This teaching of the Church was clarified at the Council of Trent. Christ is surely acting in the sacrament, but his action may receive no response. Then the result is condemnation rather than salvation.

Sacraments in Christian Life

It is time to bring together some of the things that have been said about grace, the Church, the sacraments. The Church is not the ordinary way of salvation (in the common meaning of "ordinary"), because there always have been and presumably always will be many more people outside than inside the Church. Membership in the Church is by vocation, it is response to a divine call. People outside the Church are not, by that fact, cut off from salvation and holiness. In God's plan saving grace is available to all people, though many of them will never know God or his Son explicitly. This means that it is not necessary to be a member of the visible Church to be saved; and it is not necessary to receive the seven sacraments to receive grace.

To afford the sacraments the place they are intended to have in our lives, we have to discard the idea that they are the exclusive means to obtain certain grace effects. Thousands of anonymous saints past and present never received any of the seven ritual sacraments. But by admitting the holiness of these people we admit that they received the grace effect belonging to the sacraments.

The Council of Trent reaffirmed the traditional teaching about "sacraments of desire." There is a slight confusion of terminology in this expression, since a sacrament means something visible and desire is internal. But the meaning is clear: the effects of some sacraments can be received by a proper desire and intention alone. Trent singled out three such sacraments of desire, Baptism, Penance and the Eucharist, but theologians say in addition that only two, Matrimony and Holy Orders, cannot be received by desire, because these involve the public cooperation of another person or the Church.

The graces of the sacraments, especially of the Eucharist, are needed for the progress of the life of faith. These graces are not bound to the ritual sacraments. Wherever a person responds eagerly to God's gift of himself, grace enters his life according to his need. Usually frequent reception of the sacraments means the deepening and strengthening of divine life; but this is also possible for the person who for various reasons lives and prays faithfully without knowing of the sacraments. If the maxim "the more sacraments the more grace" were true, the Church would command frequent reception of the sacraments; this she has never done. She urges frequency and a good disposition.

In order that the sacred liturgy may produce its full effect, it is necessary that the faithful come to it with proper dispositions, that their thoughts match their words, and that they cooperate with divine grace lest they receive it in vain (*Sacrosanctum Concilium*, no. 11).

If a person can live holily without the sacraments, why bother to receive them? What are the sacraments for? Sacraments make our faith more intense and tangible by giving it expression in external acts in the company of others who share our faith. We may profess belief in prayer, in service of others, in love, but this belief will fade if it is not given exercise. A man and wife do not have to express their love to one another every waking moment, but unless they do so frequently, their love can fade and wither. In one sense the sacraments are not necessary for union with God and salvation, but in another they are, for the gift of divine life needs to be expressed and nourished constantly.

The sacraments bring into focus—"sacramentalize"— the mystery of divine mercy alive in the community of faith. In the Eucharist one offers in ritual communion with other believers the sacrifice of redemption each of them is constantly offering in hidden ways. In Reconciliation, one celebrates the forgiveness and peace of Christ which is always being poured forth on repentant sinners. Anointing brings divine healing to light in a different way when a believer is sick.

Even the "one-time" sacraments have a present significance that keeps them from being simply historical events of the past. Baptism, as Paul expresses it, is insertion into the death of Christ to begin a continuing process of union with him in the paschal mystery. The rite of Baptism marks the beginning of life in the Church, but the graces of the saving event signified are obtained by prayer, sacrifice, fidelity to duty. The whole Church sacramentalizes this baptismal process at the Easter Vigil. The ex-

ternal effects of Matrimony and Orders can be traced
to definite dates, but the bestowal of the grace of these
sacraments accompanies the living of the sacramental
sign continually. Confirmation celebrates the missionary
vocation of the Christian under the living action of the
Spirit.

God's blessing of grace and forgiveness is bestowed
ideally within the visible Church of Christ. But there is
no limit to the free gift of a Father who wills to save.
Grace is imparted according to God's saving will and the
receptiveness it finds among men.

Word and Sacrament

It is necessary at this point to draw more clearly the
lines of connection between the word of God and the
sacraments that have been hinted at along the way.
Briefly, the seven sacraments are the most significant
instances of the proclamation of the word of God in
the Church. Word and sacrament were always wedded
together in early teaching. St. Augustine called the sacrament a *verbum visibile*, a visible word. Vatican Council
II, in its Constitution on Divine Revelation, drew a
strong parallel between the Bible and the Eucharist:

> The Church has always venerated the divine Scrip-
> tures just as she venerates the body of the Lord, since
> from the table of both the word of God and of the
> body of Christ she unceasingly receives and offers
> to the faithful the bread of life, especially in the
> sacred liturgy (no. 21).

Historical developments in Western Christianity ob-
scured the radical unity between word and sacrament.
The most serious rupture occurred at the Reformation.
The separation of word and sacrament became enshrined
in the very divisions of the Christian beliefs. Protestant-

ism, with its battle cry of *sola Scriptura* (Scripture alone),
became the Church of the word; while Catholicism, raising the banner of *ex opere operato,* became the Church of
the sacraments. The doctrine and life of both Christian
groups felt the debilitating effects of this separation for
the next four hundred years. It has been only in the irenic
atmosphere of the recent ecumenical movement that
Protestant and Catholic theologians have been able to
assess the damage of the word-sacrament separation. As a
result, Protestants are becoming more conscious of the
need for sacrament, and Catholics are becoming more
alert to the place of the word.

The question of ministerial priesthood was treated at
both the Council of Trent and Vatican Council II. Their
different starting-points illustrate the change of emphasis
during the intervening years. Trent defined the priesthood in terms of sacramental ministry: ". . . The power
of consecrating, offering and administering his body and
blood, as also of forgiving and retaining sins" (*Denz.*
1764). Vatican II speaks of the "ministry of the word,"
stating that the "primary duty" of priests is "the proclamation of the gospel of God to all" (*Presbyterorum
Ordinis,* no. 4).

This ministry of the word is not a return to the old
categories of division. The word of God is not confined
to the Bible or to preaching. It is carried out in many
ways, by deed as well as word, and culminates in the sacraments. The ministry of the word *includes* the ministry
of the sacraments, because the seven sacraments of the
Church are precisely the highest instances of the proclamation of the word of God in the Church. When the
worshiper at Communion says, "Only say the word, and
I shall be healed," the word he is talking about at the
moment is the Eucharist and his reception of it, a sacramental focus of Christ's healing presence.

There is a difference between the proclamation of

the word of God in a Scripture reading and the celebration of the word as one of the seven sacraments of the Church, but it is a difference of intensity, not of kind. The power of the word is in both instances the Holy Spirit, sanctifying grace. In both cases, grace is always available, but the divine effect is uncertain because it depends on the hidden disposition of the listener or recipient. But in the seven Words or Sacraments of the Church, the expected effect is definitely described: the word is focused. Baptism has an effect not expected of the Eucharist; Anointing an effect not expected of Orders, and so forth. In the reading of Scripture, a saving effect is expected, but we cannot expect it with precision. We do not have it specified as in the seven great proclamations of the Church.

READING SUGGESTIONS

Hellwig, Monika. *The Meaning of the Sacraments.* Dayton: Pflaum/Standard, 1972.

Roguet, A. M. *Christ Acts Through the Sacraments.* Collegeville, Minn.: The Liturgical Press, 1954.

Sarno, Ronald A. *Let Us Proclaim the Mystery of Faith.* Denville, N. J.: Dimension Books, 1970.

Schillebeeckx, Edward. *Christ the Sacrament of the Encounter with God.* New York: Sheed and Ward, 1963.

CHAPTER EIGHT

THE EUCHARIST-WORD

In the day to day life of most Catholics, "receiving the sacraments" means receiving the sacraments of Eucharist and Reconciliation. The renewal of sacramental liturgy, preaching, listening to the word of God will have its widest effects in terms of these two sacraments. Every Catholic's spirituality will have to give them a central place. They will be singled out now for special reflection, the Eucharist, "source and apex of the whole work of preaching the gospel" (*Presbyterorum Ordinis*, no. 5) in this chapter, the sacrament of Reconciliation in the next.

The Constitution on the Sacred Liturgy presented a broad vision of the Eucharist:

> At the Last Supper, on the night when he was betrayed, our Savior instituted the Eucharistic Sacrifice of his Body and Blood. He did this in order to perpetuate the sacrifice of the Cross throughout the centuries until he should come again, and so to entrust to his beloved spouse, the Church, a memorial of his death and resurrection: a sacrament of love, a sign of unity, a bond of charity, a paschal banquet in which Christ is consumed, the mind is filled with grace, and a pledge of future glory is given to us (no. 47).

The terms of this statement should not be overlooked.

The Mass perpetuates the "sacrifice of the Cross," which is not, however, identified only with the death on Calvary. It is a memorial of "death and resurrection," "a paschal banquet." The Eucharist is not divided into sacrifice and sacrament, as sometimes happens with a distinction between consecration and communion, but the whole rite is a "sacrament of love."

Christ's sacrifice cannot be limited to any one action of his life, even his crucifixion, though we find it convenient to do so in ordinary conversation. In its broadest terms, this sacrifice means the saving activity of Christ taken as a whole, God's becoming man in order to save men. It is the one word of salvation. The redemptive incarnation was motivated and carried forth by the perfect love and obedience at its heart: Jesus Christ's love of his Father and of us, and his obedience to the Father's will even to death for us. "There is no greater love than this: to lay down one's life for one's friends" (Jn 15:13). Every act of Jesus' earthly life was part of this sacrifice, summed up in the ultimate act of redemption, his death-resurrection.

We are speaking here, as we have earlier, of the death and resurrection as a single event of redemption. The Fathers of the Church spoke of this saving act as the *transitus* of Jesus, or his passage from death to life. His *transitus* recalls and "super-fulfills" the key redemptive act of the Old Testament, the Exodus.

Much confusion about the Mass as sacrifice has arisen because of our speaking loosely of the "repetition" of Calvary in an unbloody manner on our altars. Protestants have accused Catholics of trying to repeat what cannot be repeated. This quarrel is to a great extent a dispute about terms. It is certainly true that the Epistle to the Hebrews, which is the only explicit treatment in the New Testament of the sacrificial character of Christ's redemptive work, emphasizes the unrepeatable quality of Christ's sacrifice.

> Christ did not enter into a sanctuary made by hands, a mere copy of the true one; he entered heaven itself that he might appear before God now on our behalf. Not that he might offer himself there again and again, as the high priest enters year after year into the sanctuary with blood that is not his own; if that were so, he would have had to suffer death over and over from the creation of the world. But now he has appeared at the end of the ages to take away sins once for all by his sacrifice (Heb 9:24-26).

We would certainly be mistaken to believe that Christ sacrifices *anew* at each Mass. Jesus' once-for-all sacrifice can never be repeated. It has brought redemption to the world perfectly and finally.

The Heart of the Sacrifice

Because Jesus Christ is divine as well as human, his sacrifice is eternal. As historical events, the death on the cross and the resurrection are time-tied and can never happen again or even be made present at any future time. But the heart-reality of these events, the saving act of Christ in love and obedience, is present eternally and perfectly in the living Risen Lord. It is always present before the throne of the Father and by his great gift is always available to us. "Jesus offered one sacrifice for sins and took his seat forever at the right hand of God" (Heb 10:12).

As Christians we are dedicated to offering the sacrifice of Christ to the Father together with him. Our whole life as followers of Christ is to be a gradual entering into this sacrifice, making it our own. In other words, this means that we are to mold ourselves in his image, striving to give flesh in our own lives to that attitude of love and obedience which found perfect expression in the saving sacrifice of Jesus.

This is not a work that can be relegated to certain hours of the day or of the week. Jesus was busy at this sacrifice all through his life, not merely when it culminated in death-resurrection. Everything we do—our work, prayer, service, love, gratitude—helps us grow into this Christian sacrifice of love and obedience. Sacrifice in this sense is not this or that act of self-denial, but a way of life, a twenty-four hour job with no vacation.

The sacrifice we share and into which we are growing minute by minute is made present and available to us in a special way when we come together for the sole purpose of encountering God in worship, celebrating the mystery at the center of our life. Christ's sacrifice, eternally and perfectly present before the Father, is made available for us in sacrament at any moment of history. It is given to us in a common form that any person can understand: as a meal shared among friends. All our sacrifices of the day, all that we have and are, are placed on the altar to be taken by the Risen Lord into his own eternal offering. And then we share in the offering by partaking of his body and blood, which links us into a new bond of union, a new covenant, with one another in him.

Jesus used covenant language when he instituted the Eucharist at the Last Supper: "This is my blood, the blood of the covenant, to be poured out on behalf of many" (Mk 14:25). When the people had ratified the covenant at Sinai by their public profession, Moses sprinkled half the blood of the sacrificial victim on the altar, half on the people. God and the people were thus united symbolically. Then Moses and the elders shared the covenant meal (Ex 24:1-11).

In the blood of Jesus Christ, the lamb of sacrifice, God and the people are united more dramatically and more thoroughly by the eternal bond of the Holy Spirit. This is the new covenant Jeremiah had foretold:

> The days are coming, says the Lord, when I will make a new covenant with the house of Israel and the house of Judah. It will not be like the covenant I made with their fathers the day I took them by the hand to lead them forth from the land of Egypt; for they broke my covenant, and I had to show myself their master, says the Lord. But this is the covenant which I will make with the house of Israel after those days, says the Lord. I will place my law within them, and write it upon their hearts; I will be their God, and they shall be my people (Jr 31:31-33).

The covenant meal of the Eucharist celebrates this union and reinforces it.

For Paul, the Eucharist is the "Lord's Supper," where the Church reveals itself as the community of the new covenant. Christians united in the risen Lord form the "body of Christ" (1 Cor 6:15-20; 12:12-27). The Eucharist is the body of Christ, the source and center of the union of the members with Christ and with one another. "Because the loaf of bread is one, we, many though we are, are one body, for we all partake of the one loaf" (1 Cor 10:17). Sharing the body and blood of Jesus is communion (*koinonia*), holy communion with one another in the body of Christ (10:16). Eating and drinking unworthily is a profanation of the Eucharistic body of the Lord and of the community (11:27-29).

Unlike the Synoptics, John does not represent the Last Supper as a Passover meal, nor does he record the words of Eucharistic institution. His Eucharistic teaching comes through especially in Chapter Six of the Gospel.

This chapter begins with the multiplication of the loaves (6:1-15) and ends with a teaching on the Eucharist (especially 6:51-58).

In his dialogue with the Jews, Jesus first calls himself the "bread of life" as the revelation of the Father fulfilling the yearnings of Old Testament expectation (vv. 35-50). Suddenly his listeners find that he is going further than they can: "How can he give us his flesh to eat?" (v. 52). Jesus himself is the living bread. To have life, one must eat his flesh and drink his blood. Jesus connects the Eucharist with his redemptive death: "The bread I will give is my flesh, for the life of the world" (v. 51). Through the Eucharistic body of Jesus the believer has a share in the life of God the Father (v. 57).

Two Mistakes

Worshipers may fall into two serious mistakes about the Eucharistic sacrifice. The first error is to be so overawed by the grandeur of the Mass that we see it as something almost automatic, a rite giving glory to God simply by its valid execution. The second mistake is to suppose that the sacrificial worship of the Christian is limited to the liturgy, and that when a believer has not participated in the Mass, he has not offered the sacrifice of Christ.

The idea that the Mass has an automatic effect regardless of the participation of believers is the misunderstanding of the axiom *ex opere operato* we discussed earlier in connection with the meaning of the sacraments. This implies that when a sacramental rite has been correctly performed, a saving act of Christ, infinite in effect, is thereby produced. Thus whenever the Mass rite is performed by an ordained priest, God is glorified and saving grace is poured forth for living and dead. This justifies the repetition of the Mass indiscriminately, and except for current Church discipline to the contrary, it would be a good thing to have priests do nothing but offer Mass from

morning to night. This argument is attractive but it is
wrong; it is basically the same fallacy of "repetition" dis-
owned by the Epistle to the Hebrews.

The theological axiom means that Christ guarantees
that his sacrifice will be sacramentally available when the
Mass is correctly performed, but it does not promise an
automatic saving effect. As Christ's ever-present act of
redemption, the sacrifice is indeed infinite, but exists
whether the Mass is offered or not. Christ's sacrifice is not
renewed in the Mass; nothing is or could be added to
what is eternally and perfectly present. But it is made
sacramentally available for our participation.

The Mass is for us, not for the Father and the Son who
have no need of it. The sacrifice is brought into time sacramentally at definite moments so that we, the Church,
can join ourselves to it and make it our own. It is our
great privilege, and at the same time our great responsibility, to be able to speak of Christ's sacrifice as "our sacrifice": "Pray, brethren, that *our* sacrifice may be acceptable to God, the almighty Father." It is our responsibility
because the Mass as an historical action has limited effect
depending on the participation of the worshipers. From
this point of view the Mass is different every time it is
offered. If the sacrifice of Christ does not become our
sacrifice, that is, if there is no involvement of human
faith, the Mass can do nothing for God's glory or man's
salvation. The mere multiplication of Masses serves no
redemptive purpose.

> Like the passion of Christ itself, the sacrifice of the
> Mass, though offered for all, has no effect except in
> those united to the passion of Christ by faith and
> charity. To these it brings a greater or less benefit in
> proportion to their devotion (*Instruction on the Wor-
> ship of the Eucharistic Mystery*, 1967, no. 12).

The second mistake is to identify the offering of

Christ's sacrifice solely with the Fucharist. This restricts our life of worship to a very narrow base.

> The spiritual life is not confined to participation in the liturgy. The Christian is assuredly called to pray with his brethren, but he must also enter into his chamber to pray to the Father in secret; indeed, according to the teaching of the Apostle Paul, he should pray without ceasing. We learn from the same Apostle that we must always carry about in our body the dying of Jesus, so that the life of Jesus too may be made manifest in our bodily frame. This is why we ask the Lord in the sacrifice of the Mass that, "receiving the offering of the spiritual victim," he may fashion us for himself "as an eternal gift" (*Sacrosanctum Concilium*, no. 12).

There are myriad ways of putting on the sacrifice of Christ. One day it may be a sick child to care for. Or it may take the form of sharing time with a troubled friend. The reading of the Bible, private prayer, different acts of self-denial, deepen in us the attitudes necessary for becoming loving and obedient in Christ's image. Everything we do outside of Mass, in fact, should be remote preparation for the moment we make explicit the offering we are always living. Looked at this way, there is no absolute rule about the frequency of the Mass in our lives. It should be balanced with our other obligations and possibilities in offering the sacrifice of Christ. A mother would not leave her baby unprotected in order to attend Mass. We would hope that daily Mass-goers are more conscious of Christ's sacrifice in their lives than are those who participate sporadically, but it is not necessarily so. Participation in the sacrifice of Christ is demanded at every moment, whether we are at Mass or not.

The Mass in Context

Sadly, we sometimes use attendance at Mass as an escape from momentarily more demanding forms of offering. It is then that we reveal ourselves as "spiritual gluttons" at heart, convinced that we automatically "get more out of" the Mass than any other form of prayer or Christian living. We may excuse ourselves from being with a person who needs our help for the sake of a second Mass or one to which we are not bound; or use it as a substitute for the private prayer or spiritual reading which at this particular moment may be really more demanding and important to our living of Christ's sacrifice. It is here that we weaken the effect of the Mass in our lives and diminish its importance, by simply removing it from any meaningful connection with other ways of sharing the sacrifice. This is not meant to deny the value of frequent participation in the Mass. But when the Mass becomes something we "go through" to salve our consciences, there is a deadening of our Eucharistic sensibilities until it is harder and harder to worship eagerly at Mass anytime.

The Mass must be taken for what it is within the context of our whole life of worship. It is an intense form of community prayer demanding active participation and continual mental alertness. In this it is different from more tranquil forms of prayer like the Liturgy of the Hours, meditation, and many private devotions. We can repeat these prayers over and over again, even several times a day, but full participation in the Mass involves a spiritual intensity which argues against its constant repetition. It is up to the individual Christian to determine the frequency of the Mass in his offering of the sacrifice of Christ. The Church, recognizing our limitations, encourages frequent participation in the Mass, but demands it only once a week. This Mass obligation starts before the rite begins. Let the faithful come to the liturgy inwardly prepared, the Council admonished, "that their thoughts match their words, and that they cooperate with divine grace lest they receive it in vain" (*Sacrosanctum Concilium*, no. 11).

Preparation for Mass

Pride of place in the renewal of the Mass is given to this interior preparation, but that is not all there is to it. The Council decree and subsequent instructions have pointed out the importance of the training and the personal involvement of the ministers in the preparation of biblical texts, the selection of participation materials, and the provision for liturgical vestments and vessels and the physical surroundings conducive to celebration.

The chief personal obligation here belongs to the celebrant, who has the task of creating a sense of community prayer and evoking the full participation of all the worshipers. The celebrant's role seemed formerly to consist mostly in the impersonal execution of standard formulas, but the Church assures us in her recent pronouncements that the celebrant's function is closer to an art. He must study the needs of his congregation and plan the best way to bring to the worshipers the message proclaimed on each occasion. If he brings only rubrics to the Mass, he will be giving stale bread to those who come to be fed.

Others too are uniquely involved in creating the context for the Mass. The reader should be well prepared and conscious of the power of the word he proclaims. Christ forms his community for celebration of the mysteries by this word; the reading must not be dull or stumbling. The role of the music director demands special care, for he can use his talent and the materials at his disposal to lift the community into a celebrating mood. The music at Mass is designed to intensify the alertness of the participants and to echo the word in forging the group into a worshiping unity.

The Eucharistic renewal inaugurated by the Council has already made a difference in the life of the Church. But few Catholics, of whatever theological persuasion, are completely satisfied with the reform we have achieved to date. The Council program for renewal of the Mass relies heavily on instilling in worshipers the attitude of celebration and a sense of community. Built into the new ordinary of the Mass are opportunities for more spontaneity, especially on the part of the celebrant, and rites like the sign of peace to give concrete expression to the unity of the worshiping congregation.

Behind our impatience with the renewal of the Mass often lies uncertainty about what the Council really intended to do. Those who are truly concerned should read the documents again carefully with attention to the historical background of the pronouncements and the theology they express. And then we must listen to the demands Christ is making on each of us personally, to insure that when we participate in the Mass we are intensely involved in making his sacrifice our own.

READING SUGGESTIONS

Vatican Council II, *Constitution on the Sacred Liturgy (Sacrosanctum Concilium)*; and Sacred Congregation of Rites, *Instruction on the Worship of the Eucharistic Mystery (Eucharisticum Mysterium, 1967)*, in Austin Flannery, ed. *The Conciliar and Post Conciliar Documents.* Northport, New York: Costello, 1975.

Champlin, Joseph M. *The Mass in a World of Change.* Notre Dame: Ave Maria Press, 1973.

Palmer, Paul F. *Sacraments and Worship.* Westminster, Md.: Newman Press, 1955.

Vagaggini, Cyprian. *Theological Dimensions of the Liturgy.* Collegeville, Minn.: Liturgical Press, 1976.

CHAPTER NINE

THE WORD OF RECONCILIATION

A beautiful versicle in the Liturgy of the Hours reads: "Father, you sent your Son to reconcile the world to you by his blood. Enable us to be ministers of reconciliation." It is a reflection of Paul's teaching on reconciliation in Second Corinthians:

> If anyone is in Christ, he is a new creation. The old order has passed away; now all is new! All this has been done by God, who has reconciled us to himself through Christ and has given us the ministry of reconciliation. I mean that God, in Christ, was reconciling the world to himself, not counting men's transgressions against them, and that he has entrusted the message of reconciliation to us. This makes us ambassadors for Christ, God as it were appealing through us. We implore you, in Christ's name: be reconciled to God! (2 Cor 5:17-20).

There is a wide-reaching program in the Church at the present time to help us understand and deepen in ourselves this mystery of reconciliation. "Renewal and Reconciliation" was the theme of the Holy Year; the sacrament we have known as Confession or Penance has been given the official name of Sacrament of Reconciliation. This emphasis has not been decided by the flip of a coin. The

Church of Vatican II is searching for ways to focus all the various elements of our faith-life into a few central channels. The theme of reconciliation is as central as you can get. The word of God in Jesus is a word of reconciliation. "God has given us the wisdom to understand fully the mystery, the plan he has pleased to decree in Christ, to be carried out in the fullness of time: namely, to bring all things in the heavens and on earth into one under Christ's headship" (Ep 1:9-10).

Three Reconciliations

The two biblical statements quoted so far both deal with reconciliation, but they are talking about two different aspects of it. The first speaks of reconciliation to the Father through the Son, the goal of all; the second speaks of reconciliation among men. There is a third kind of reconciliation often referred to in Scripture as the forgiveness of sin. It is the reconciliation that takes place inside a person, the closing of the gap between what we want to be and what we are (Rm 7:15-25). Though reconciliation happens on all three levels at the same time, this is the fundamental healing that makes the thorough reconciliation possible.

The total reconciliation of man with God, with other men, and with himself is known in the Bible as *shalom* or peace. Man is helpless to achieve this on his own. It is the kind of peace that the world cannot give. The good news in Jesus Christ is that this deep and lasting peace, this reconciliation, has been given as a free gift from God and we Christians are its ministers.

> All this is the work of the kindness of our God;
>   he, the Dayspring, shall visit us in his mercy
> To shine on those who sit in darkness and in the
>   shadow of death,
>   to guide our feet into the way of peace (Lk 1:78-79).

God's work of reconciliation, and our ministry of it, are active in every sacrament of the Church and in every faithful Christian act. It is highlighted and climaxed in the sacrament of Reconciliation. Most of us will find out what reconciliation means in the rest of our lives through the few moments of encounter with Jesus in this sacrament. We will rejoice more and more in the rich truth of the words "Go in peace."

No sooner had the Council decreed the renewal of the sacrament of Penance than confessions began to decline everywhere. People gave all kinds of reasons, old and new, for avoiding this sacrament. Old reasons included the classic "Why should I confess to a man when I can tell God directly?," charges against the impersonality of the confessional box, and the statement that confession seems to have no effect in the penitent's life.

The reform of the liturgy itself has been responsible for some new reasons. The penitential rite of the Mass, if it means anything, involves the Church's ministry of forgiveness. The same is true of communal celebrations of the sacrament, with or without private confession. If Christ forgives me here, why must I still confess. Besides, Catholics are realizing that the Church has always taught that sins can be forgiven by acts of contrition, the reception of other sacraments, and by sacramentals. Mixed with all this is uncertainty about the nature of sin and the sinfulness of particular acts. It used to be clear what was a sin and what was not, but now much more is attributed to the personal and circumstantial.

This crisis of the sacrament is really a part of the renewal itself, and in the long run will be seen as a positive development. There are good and true religious instincts involved in the criticisms people have been making. They have pushed the Church to a thorough renewal of the catechesis and practice of the sacrament.

Sin, Forgiveness, Sacrament

It is as harmful to equate sins with sin as it is to equate prayers with prayer. Sin is not a black mark, it is not something that can be collected in stacks, like a commodity off the devil's grocery shelf. This is the mistake of a "priest-as-wastebasket" syndrome, which sees sins as acts or omissions that can be carried to the confessional and deposited as so much dead weight. The priest unloads the freight, and the sinner makes a fresh start.

Individual acts of wrongdoing do indicate what our sin is, but a sinful condition is not just the sum of transgressions. Maybe a better word for our trouble is "sinfulness," something deepseated that keeps us turning our head in the wrong direction. It may be that the real problem is not unkind remarks, or impure thoughts, or distractions in prayer, but something more basic, like selfishness, grasping for glory, dishonesty. When individual sins are confessed without touching the sinfulness that undergirds them, confession is a soothing massage, not a treatment to bring healing.

Though the Church makes rules for the reception of the Sacrament of Reconciliation and requires all mortal sins to be confessed, she has never tied forgiveness of sin to the sacrament. It is a matter between the sinner and God. We can be forgiven even the most serious sins outside the sacrament by an interior act of sorrow, which we call the act of contrition. The distinction between "perfect" and "imperfect" contrition has caused a lot of trouble, seeming to put immediate forgiveness out of reach for most people. But (perfect) contrition is within the reach of anyone who can make the act of contrition sincerely intending sorrow. Sorrow for sin is not the same as *feeling* sorry; whoever wants to be sorry for sin is forgiven. "If we acknowledge our sins," writes St. John, "he who is just can be trusted to forgive our sins and cleanse us from every wrong" (1 Jn 1:9). God makes only one demand, that we admit our sin and cast ourselves into his care.

When Jesus came into the upper room on the evening of the resurrection, he brought a great gift. "Peace be with you," he said. "Receive the Holy Spirit; if you forgive men's sins they are forgiven them; if you hold them bound, they are held bound" (Jn 20:22-23). The sacrament of Reconciliation is a "sacrament of growth" for the healing of the sinner. Sinfulness builds up over a long time, often years, and is not ordinarily corrected overnight. The return to strength is slow.

In this sacrament, Jesus reaches out to me in his ministry of forgiveness and healing. He offers me his own Spirit of peace, self-acceptance, reconciliation, joy. For this meeting, I must be concerned to present myself, not just a list of sins. My actions help me know who and where I am in myself and with Christ, and so I need to reveal them to the confessor. But I must present as complete a picture as is needed. Any deception here is silly; it is not my catalogue of sins or my mask that needs healing, but me.

"I failed to say my morning prayers five times" may be an adequate statement of my spiritual situation. But maybe I haven't prayed much at all and should admit it: "I find it awfully easy to forget about God most of the time and live mainly for myself." Good things as well as bad constitute a sinner's condition, progress as well as loss of ground, and the confessor is there to help the penitent see himself clearly. The "penance" is meant to continue the process of healing begun or reinforced in the sacrament.

Why Confess to a Man?

This perennial question is based on a valid conviction: We do not have to go through men to receive God's forgiveness. He is as close as our heart. So it would seem that if there is an offense between my neighbor and me, we could admit sorrow to one another privately and individually to God and thus put an end to the affair. The catch is that sin is bigger than us. It breaks out beyond our small circle and has effects we can never control.

When I sin, I knowingly contradict the truth, the right, that I have established as a rule for living deep within myself. This is so whatever my value may be, and whether I call the self-betrayal sin or not. Sin brings me down a notch. I am always less a person because of the decision that cuts a path around the truth. I become dangerous, because whoever meets me is meeting an injured person, and the only way I can draw is down. If you are weak where I am, my sinfulness may draw you down; then maybe my sin in you will draw somebody else down, and the process will go on and on. No sin is private; it will ripple out across the world, breeding more and more sin. My sin may finally erupt in a war somewhere, or in an act of terrorism, or in a street killing. None of us can say, at this moment, that our sins have finally run their course. For all we know, our forgotten sins are still cutting their way through the world.

In denying his personal truth, the sinner splits himself inside, and at the same time denies God, the faithful and true. He breaks faith with the community of all men seeking the truth, and especially with the Church, the nearer community of faith within which he lives. The result is alienation, a feeling of being misdirected or aimless, cut off from the good, outcast.

Personal sorrow and settling of differences can never reach far enough to heal all these effects of sin. No human can take it upon himself to assure himself or another, "It's all right." But God, who sees all and is over all, can utter the word of reconciliation. In the sacrament, Christ lifts the burden from my shoulders, taking on himself my sin and its effects. He helps me forgive myself, and begins to make me into a whole person again. The sacrament of Reconciliation proclaims healing of interior wounds. The priest acts as Christ's minister and the representative of the Church in proclaiming the divinely reliable word of peace: "It's all right. You are forgiven and accepted back just as you are. Your sins no longer condemn you. You are loved."

The penitent is still a sinner, but he has accepted himself in weakness and been accepted by Christ in power. Each confession is a new setting out on the pilgrimage toward fullness in Christ. When the woman taken in adultery was brought to Jesus he did not deny her guilt nor the seriousness of her sin, and he did not indicate that she was thoroughly changed by encountering him. But he accepted her in her weakness and encouraged her to begin anew: "I do not condemn you. You may go. But from now on, avoid this sin" (Jn 8:11).

The how and the how often of confession is for the penitent and the confessor to decide. The sacrament of Reconciliation should be celebrated regularly according to the natural rhythms of a person's life: work, school, Church year. The times between celebrations of this sacrament should ordinarily be long enough to be significant and short enough to be remembered. To say "I have nothing to confess" is to admit confusing sinful actions with deepdown sin. There is enough sinfulness behind the "same old things" to satisfy the requirements of the sacrament anytime. If we approach the sacrament with the proper disposition, our particular offenses have probably been forgiven already. But we come to be reconciled and healed.

The Power of the Word

The Church has been arranging for the generous use of the Bible in the renewal of all her liturgical celebrations. The sacraments are proclamations of the word of

God, instruments of its grace and power. The use of the written word intensifies the presence of Christ. The scriptural passages unlock sealed doors of the heart by the spiritual power of the word. In any use of the Bible there is also instruction to enlighten the mind with saving truth. In the sacraments this power and enlightenment combine to promote a deeper personal understanding and acceptance of the mystery celebrated.

There are numerous biblical passages recommended for use in the sacrament of Reconciliation, especially the gospel stories of healing and forgiveness: the paralytic, the leper, the sinful woman, the man born blind. One of the favorites, much used in communal celebrations of the sacrament, is the story of the prodigal son. It belongs with the classics of literature for its brief, simple illustration of profound truths of human life. And for our purpose, it is one of the best gospel instructions on the mystery of sin, forgiveness and reconciliation. The following comments will be read to best advantage with a Bible at hand.

A Family Story (Lk 15:11-31)

The younger son takes off impetuously with the whole world before him. All is not right with him, though he does not know it at the time. He has been selfish in thinking only of himself, having no regard for the needs and feelings of his father or his brother. He thinks he can be completely independent and do his own thing.

It takes a crisis to open his eyes, and he sees the three-fold rupture—from God, from his father (and brother) and within himself: "I have sinned against God and against you; I no longer deserve to be called your son." He is still a long way from reconciliation, though. Even after all these years, he does not know his father very well. "Treat me like one of your hired hands." He doubts his father's love, expecting a grudging acceptance and a place on the fringes from here on out. But his father has been waiting and watching for him every day, so that "while he was still a long way off, his father caught sight of him." The father does not compose himself and wait for the moment of encounter, choosing the stern words of a righteous judge. "He ran out to meet him, threw his arms around his neck, and kissed him."

The sinful son does not even have to come all the way back home before his father is there with all his love. His is not a prove-yourself-first stance; it is rather wide-open-love without question. As much as we rejoice in this kind of love for ourselves, we are usually jealous when it is showered on others. "The elder son grew angry at this and would not go in." We can hear his mind working. This is the squirt who left me with all the work, who made a fool of himself and lost our hard-earned money. It doesn't make sense to receive him back with open arms. Make him pay. See if he has really reformed.

"His father came out and began to plead with him." The father loves both his sons. "You are with me always, and everything I have is yours." He wants them both to be happy through the freedom of love. His love makes it possible for them to love. Any holding back stifles the lover as surely as it harms the loved. "We had to celebrate and rejoice! This brother of yours was dead and has come back to life. He was lost and is found." The return of the lost son, this reconciliation, is more important than anything else. It is more important than the money he lost, the sins he committed, the feelings he hurt. It is a resurrection.

This parable is misnamed. It is really the story of the Prodigal Father. A prodigal is one who squanders. This father gives away love beyond reason. He is like God, our prodigal Father. Jesus' parable is a proclamation of God's no-strings-attached love. He loved us first, so much so that he sent his Son to die for us before we could do anything to deserve it. "It is rare that anyone should lay down his life for a just man, though it is barely possible that for a good man someone may have the courage to die. It is precisely in this that God proves his love for us: that while we were still sinners, Christ died for us" (Rm 5:7-8). This radical love of the Father is the basis of reconciliation. It gives sinners the heart to seek forgiveness.

As ministers of reconciliation, the disciples of Jesus are given the commission of spreading the news of this marvelous love of God. We tend to be more squeamish with God's love than he is. "God will forgive you if you do this or that; if you perform this act of penance; if you prove that you have reformed." Our message is not the original good news; it is only fair news: God will forgive you if. But our Father is completely generous. Very little was asked of the son in the parable, and very little is asked of us. We just have to turn around and start back, and immediately the Father is there, throwing his arms around us and bringing us home.

READING SUGGESTIONS

Bishops' Committee on the Liturgy. *Study Text* 4: *Rite of Penance*. Washington: USCC, 1975.

Buckley, Francis J. *I Confess. The Sacrament of Penance Today. Notre Dame*: Ave Maria Press, 1972.

Haering, Bernard. *Shalom: Peace; The Sacrament of Reconciliation*. New York: Farrar, Straus and Giroux, 1968.

Palmer, Paul F., ed. *Sacraments and Forgiveness*. Westminster, Md.: Newman Press, 1959.

CHAPTER TEN

WORD AND PRAYER

In relating the word of God to the life of the believer, the New Testament treats the word like a diamond being turned slowly to sparkle in the light of the sun. It is first of all the agent of new life. "The Father wills to bring us to birth with a word spoken in truth" (Jm 1:18). "Your rebirth has come, not from a destructible but from an indestructible seed, through the living and enduring word of God" (1 P 1:23). This word is identified by Peter as the "gospel which was preached to you," centering in the great word of resurrection (1 P 1:3,25). Growth in this new life depends on "holding fast to the word of life" (Ph 2:16). "Let the word of Christ dwell in you" (Col 3:16). If a Christian bases himself on the words of Jesus, his life will be a house built on rock (Mt 7:24-25). Paul tells the Thessalonians that the word of God is "at work" among them (1 Th 2:13). Timothy has been "reared in the words of faith" (1 Tm 4:6). In his missionary endeavors Paul keeps in mind that "I planted the seed and Apollos watered it, but God made it grow" (1 Cor 3:6).

This word of God has saving effect in proportion to its acceptance in the human heart. That is the message of the parable of the sower (Mk 4:1-9). When the word has no saving effect, it is no fault of the word, pregnant with saving grace; it is good seed, but the soil is not

ready to receive and nurture it. Every human life has
moments of awakening to the message of salvation. There
is no particular pattern when or how the grace of God
may strike. Paul's meeting with the risen Lord was the
last thing he had in mind on the way to Damascus. If
there is no pattern to receiving the word of God, there
is a pattern to its deepening and cultivation. The word
grows best in times of prayer.

The emphasis of this chapter will be on prayer as
listening. All types of prayer combine listening and response to the word of God. The biblical theme of the
word of God is best understood, though, in terms of
prayer as waiting and listening for the voice of the Lord.
The emphasis here is on the divine action in the transformation of the believer, and through the believer the
world. We are never to be only hearers of the word and
not doers (Jm 1:22). But waiting for the word we realize
that we are to be recipients and instruments of the Lord's
action, not the instigators of our own. "Humbly welcome
the word that has taken root in you, with its power to
save you" (Jm 1:21).

In John's Gospel, the one who is "begotten from
above" (3:3) must continue in the word, keep the word
(8:31,51); the word "abides" in the heart of the believer (5:38). Words of Jesus listened to in faith are
spirit and life (6:63). John sees the word as an active
force that "cleans" the Apostles, pruning away dead
wood from the branches (15:3); it condemns on the last
day (12:48). This active quality of the word is involved
in its description as the "sword of the spirit" (Ep 6:17),
and in the moving statement of Hebrews: "God's word
is living and effective, sharper than any two-edged sword.
It penetrates and divides soul and spirit, joints and marrow; it judges the reflections and thoughts of the heart"
(4:12). Prayer reaches out to this word, welcomes it,
gives it a home.

The Prayer of Jesus

We know quite a bit about the content of Jesus' prayer. In the Garden he spoke to God in a thoroughly new way, calling him "Abba" (Mk 14:36). In the Lord's Prayer, Jesus taught us to pray that way, too, and to ask for the coming of the kingdom (Lk 11:2-4). He broke out in praise and thanksgiving when he was misunderstood by the great but understood by the lowly (Mt 12:25-27). At the Last Supper he prayed for his Apostles and for those who would follow them in belief. He prayed for the unity of his disciples that the world might believe (Jn 17:20-21).

But the recorded prayers of Jesus are not the only teaching we have from him about prayer. His example of prayer is an instruction, too. "Rising early the next morning, he went off to a lonely place in the desert; there he was absorbed in prayer" (Mk 1:35). We have no way of knowing what Jesus' prayer consisted of that morning. He went to be by himself to be absorbed in prayer. Another time he took the apostles to be "by themselves in a deserted place" (Mk 6:32). Though the pressure of the crowds spoiled this plan, after Jesus had fed the people he "went off to the mountain to pray." This was in the evening. He came to the Apostles again in the wee hours of the morning, presumably having spent the intervening time in prayer (Mk 6:46-48).

Jesus sought solitude and time for his personal prayer. When he could not find this during the day, he found it at night. He was in special communion with his Father at these times. We know from the description of his prayer in the Garden how intense his prayer could be, and Mark describes him as being "absorbed" in prayer in the Galilean desert. We can presume that part of his prayer during this time was a searching for the will of his Father. Luke pictures Jesus as spending the whole night before choosing his Apostles "in communion with

God" (Lk 6:12); he was praying at his baptism and transfiguration, two momentous stages in his mission (Lk 3:21; 9:29). The forty-day desert prelude to his preaching ministry is described in the gospels as a time of testing by Satan. This included a search for the will of the Father.

Mary

Mary is the model of the Christian believer as faithful listener to the word of God. "At the message of the angel, the Virgin Mary received the Word of God in her heart and in her body, and gave Life to the world" (*Lumen Gentium*, no. 53). This theme, developed by the Fathers and teachers of the Church through the centuries, finds its strongest New Testament reference in the Gospel of Luke. At the Annunciation Mary accepted her vocation as mother of the Redeemer: "I am the servant of the Lord. Let it be done to me according to your word" (Lk 1:38). Elizabeth praised her for her faith: "Blest is she who trusted that the Lord's words to her would be fulfilled" (1:45). Mary could not always understand what God was doing in her life. She did not rebel, but kept all these things "in her heart" (2:51).

On one occasion when Mary and members of Jesus' family came to visit him, Jesus acted in a way that could have been taken as a slur against her and them. " 'Your mother and your brothers are standing outside and they wish to see you.' He told them in reply, 'My mother and my brothers are those who hear the word of God and act upon it' " (8:20-21). Another time a woman in the crowd tried to praise Mary for producing such a wonderful son: "Blest is the womb that bore you and the breasts that nursed you." Jesus corrected the woman: "Blest rather are they who hear the word of God and keep it" (11:28).

Jesus is not denying the worth of his mother in these episodes. But he is directing his listeners to her true worth. The infancy story has already shown how Mary listened to the word of God and kept it. She would be faithful through the crisis of Jesus' death, and after the Ascension she would be found with the Apostles, "devoted to constant prayer" and waiting for the promise from on high (Ac 1:14). It is not Mary's physical relationship to Jesus that makes her the model of all believers. It is because she is precisely the one who, in the most important way, was the faithful hearer of the word. Among the Fathers of the Church it was an axiom that Mary's beauty came from this. She was the Mother of God in her heart before she was in her body (*prius in mente quam ventre*). The Council quote is worth repeating: "At the message of the angel, the Virgin Mary received the Word of God in her heart and in her body, and gave Life to the world" (*Lumen Gentium*, no. 53).

The early Fathers delighted in seeing Mary as the model of every Christian in this attitude of receptivity for the word of God. Origen saw Baptism as the conception of the word of God in the soul:

> Just as an infant is formed in the womb, so it seems to me that the word of God is in the heart of a soul which has received the grace of baptism and then forms within itself the word of faith ever more glorious (*Homily on Exodus*, 10, 4).

St. Gregory Nazianzen speaks the same way of Christ being carried in the Christian:

> Every soul carries Christ within itself as in a womb. If the person is not transformed through a holy life, he cannot be called Christ's mother. Yet whenever you receive Christ's word within you, and let it live in your heart, and build it up with your thoughts as in the womb, then you can be called Christ's mother (*The Blind Man and Zaccheus*, 4).

St. Ambrose liked to speak of the faithful Christian as a "Mary." The believer must be faithful to the word or Christ can be miscarried.

> Not all have brought to birth, not all are perfect, not all are "Mary": for even though they have conceived Christ by the Holy Spirit, they have not all brought him to birth. There are those who thrust out the word of God, as it were miscarrying. See to it therefore that you do the will of the Father, so that you may be the mother of Christ (*Commentary on Luke,* 10:24-25).

And St. Augustine said: "When you look with wonder on what happened to Mary, you must imitate her in the depths of your own soul" (*Sermon* 191, 4).

The Church sees herself imitating Mary in this openness to the word: "The Church, contemplating Mary's mysterious sanctity, imitating her charity, and faithfully fulfilling the Father's will, becomes herself a mother by accepting God's word in faith" (*Lumen Gentium,* no. 64). She invites her children to follow Mary's "pilgrimage of faith," and to look to her as a model of humble availability to the divine call, "embracing God's saving will with a full heart" (no. 56).

The Psalms

The psalms, Israel's inspired prayers, were born of the prayerful reflection of Israel on God's acts of salvation. Many of them are much more personal than this sounds: individual meditations, responses, calls for divine assistance. This kind of prayer is found also beyond the 150 psalms of the psalter in all the prayerful poems, canticles and hymns in the biblical collection. In these, prayer and meditation in response to the word of God has become the word of God.

Most of the psalms, in the form we have them today, date from the time of the Exile (587-538 B.C.) or later. During this time of suffering when connection with the promised land and ancient religious institutions had been shattered, prayer became more spiritual among the Israelites. Observant Hebrews were driven to the essentials of scripture and prayer. By listening for the Lord's voice and pouring out his heart in psalmody, the pious Israelite could build a temple of prayer any place.

The earliest origins of the psalms lie in the liturgical celebrations of the great deeds of the Lord. One of these ancient psalms is found in Exodus 15:1-18, a hymn praising Yahweh for the defeat of the Egyptians at the Red Sea. Besides the Exodus, other favorite themes were "words of the Lord" in the Conquest and the making of the Covenant. Yahweh was God above all gods. At the time of the monarchy, psalms of enthronement and of thanksgiving for victory demonstrated the belief that Yahweh had his protective and guiding hand on Israel's kings.

The major prophets from the eighth century B.C. on found the cultic ritual in which the earlier psalms had arisen in need of purification. There was a continual tendency to add ingredients from Canaanite ritual to the cult of Yahweh. They noticed that fervent temple worship did not always go hand in hand with justice and charity (Am 4:1-5). The word of the Lord that came to these prophets was a call to return to true worship. Their poetic oracles were less reflective and glorious:

> Your hands are full of blood!
> Wash yourselves clean!
> Put away your misdeeds from before my eyes;
> cease doing evil; learn to do good.
> Make justice your aim: redress the wronged,
> hear the orphan's plea, defend the widow
> (Is 1:15-17).

The poetic prayers of Israel light a path of proclamation and response through Israel's history. The psalmists left us a pageant of faith; not simply a dead word
but an experience with a heartbeat. Real-life situations
were reacted to, wrestled with, prayed over in living
reference to divine revelation as a past and present experience. The way that Israel listened and responded to the
word of the Lord became a standard for all believers in
the biblical tradition.

The Prayer of the Heart

The notion of prayer as listening to the word of God
may sound too simple. Prayer after all is communion with
God. The psalmists were often anything but silent and
receptive. Is there danger that our passive listening will
reduce God's revelation to a monologue? Prayerful biblical listening is silent, but it is not passive. Mary was
silent in pondering the word that had been spoken to her,
but her heart was active.

There is renewed interest in all types of prayer these
days, vocal, meditative, contemplative. Forgotten strands
of the Church's prayer tradition have been recovered,
with a general deepening of prayer consciousness. The
new interest has generated a wealth of books and articles,
workshops and conferences. So much is being said about
techniques of prayer that the recognized good of this renewal is in danger of being undermined by a kind of
nervousness: Am I praying right? Should I try this new
way, or that? What if I waste my time with a prayer that
doesn't fit me, or one that doesn't please God?

St. Paul seems to have felt the same way once, or at
least he knew some people who did. He settled a lot in a
few crisp words: "We do not know how to pray as we
ought, but the Spirit himself expresses our plea in a way
that could never be put into words. He who searches
hearts knows what the Spirit means, for the Spirit pleads

with God on behalf of his people, and in accordance
with his will" (Rm 8:26-27). In other words, stop worry-
ing about the way you're praying. You have the Holy
Spirit inside you and he knows just how you should pray.
In fact, he is praying for you. Paul doesn't say prayer
isn't important, but he wants the Romans (and us) to be
concerned about the right things in prayer. The important thing is to want to pray, and to set aside time for it,
and even to try various methods and prayer exercises.
But it is wrong to be worried or frantic about prayer.
"The Spirit himself expresses our plea."

A closer look reveals that Paul is not thinking here
of prayer as something you do, but as something going
on inside you. The Christian is in a "state of prayer,"
another way of saying he is in the state of grace, because
of the presence of the Holy Spirit. Prayer has been hum-
ming in the Christian ever since Baptism. We can stop it,
but we don't have to start it. It is like a perfectly tuned
motor that is set to run through the end of time and for
all eternity.

Too often we are unaware of this inner prayer. The
treasure we carry in our heart is hidden even from us.
Prayer goes on within us without us. But when we pray
consciously we connect with this flow of love in our
depths. By the exercises and techniques of our prayer
times we dip into this current, engaging the praying
Spirit in the midst of his eternal prayer. And it is in this
way, as we bring the hidden prayer of our heart to active
life and consciousness, that our life begins to be saturated
by divine power and we experience transformation in
Christ. Other people then experience Christ in us. The
more we "pray without ceasing" (1 Th 5:17), the more
we bear the "fruit of the spirit": love, joy, peace, patience,
kindness, generosity, faith, mildness, chastity (Gal 5:
22-23). Our life becomes a sacrament of God's presence.
We evangelize by being.

The Holy Spirit

The Holy Spirit is the Prayer and the Pray-er. He eternally expresses the love between the Father and the Son, and by his indwelling presence brings us into that movement of life, or brings that movement of life into us (Jn 14:15-23). "God is the one who firmly establishes us along with you in Christ; it is he who anointed us and has sealed us, thereby depositing the first payment, the Spirit, in our hearts" (2 Cor 1:21-22). The Spirit is not the icing on the cake of our Christian life, says Paul, an added extra that makes it tastier. The Spirit is the cake. He makes everything possible. "No one can say 'Jesus is Lord' except in the Holy Spirit" (1 Cor 12:3).

The Spirit teaches us how to pray. As we would expect from the Spirit Jesus promised, the prayer he teaches us and the prayer Jesus gave us are the same. "When you pray, say: 'Father'" (Lk 11:2). "God has sent forth into our hearts the spirit of his Son which cries out 'Abba!' ('Father')" (Gal 4:6). It is the Spirit who makes us children of the Father, and who by his presence convinces us that we are not servants or slaves, but sons and daughters. "The spirit you received is not the spirit of slaves bringing fear into your lives again; it is the spirit of sons, and it makes us cry out, 'Abba, Father!' The Spirit himself and our spirit bear united witness that we are children of God" (Rm 8:14-17).

In Christian prayer we do not try to make contact with a God who is far away nor do we have to generate our prayer from a standing start. When we pray "Come, Holy Spirit" we are not calling God down out of the clouds. He is present within us and we are rather calling ourselves to wake up to his presence. "Here I stand, knocking at the door. If anyone hears me calling and opens the door, I will enter his house and have supper with him, and he with me" (Rv 3:20).

We want our heart to beat to the rhythm of the Spirit, to be attuned to the word that penetrates to the marrow. The Holy Spirit invades our consciousness and with his help we bring to expression what is going on in the depths. Sometimes he gives the "gift of tongues," and the prayer remains "unutterable" and undecipherable even as it is being expressed. This prayer may sound like gibberish to a bystander but nonetheless be a powerful personal prayer. "A man who speaks in a tongue is talking not to men but to God. No one understands him, because he utters mysteries in the Spirit" (1 Cor 14:2).

Our prayer need not be a nervous search for novelty. The Spirit is calmly praying within us, always ready to guide and perfect our slightest inclination toward God. An attempt at prayer is prayer. The different methods of prayer help us open up to the life inside, to hear the word God is speaking to our heart, and to respond in love. Because our prayer is "Abba," learning to pray is the same as learning to be a child. Layers of hardheartedness have covered up the child inside. Pride, independence and fear make it impossible to say "Father." Here, too, the Spirit helps us as we try to strip away the layers of sin to get to our heart where he is waiting. Our asceticism goes from the outside to the inside, what the spiritual writers have called a progress from the purgative stage through the illuminative to the unitive.

Mary pondered the word of God in her life. She took it down into her heart and let it grow, and gave life to the world. Listening prayer brings us to the center of ourselves. The mystics stress the quietness and simplicity of this prayer. It is union with God speaking from "outside" in the happenings of life, but most of all it is communion through the Spirit within. At its highest stage prayer is silent, filled with the word.

READING SUGGESTIONS

Farrell, Edward J. *Prayer is a Hunger*. Denville, N. J.: Dimension Books, 1972.

French, R. M., tr. *The Way of a Pilgrim*. New York: Seabury Press, 1952.

Louf, Andre. *Teach Us To Pray*. Chicago: Franciscan Herald Press, 1975.

Rahner, Hugo. *Our Lady and the Church*. London: Darton, Longman and Todd, 1961.

CHAPTER ELEVEN

PROCLAIMING THE WORD OF GOD

Our lives have been transformed by the many ways the word of God's salvation has been proclaimed to us. The word has an effect, it does not return void. Neither does the word remain idle. It is a living message to be passed on from person to person, a treasure of grace, a call to faith and life. "Faith comes through hearing, and what is heard is the word of Christ" (Rm 10:17). Those who have given the word a home in their hearts cannot hoard it there behind closed doors. They must pass it on, proclaim the message to others who have not yet been so fortunate.

In an earlier chapter we spoke about the biblical doctrine of the universality of grace, a doctrine strongly reiterated and developed at Vatican II. Saving grace is not limited to members of the Church but is available in fullness for all men wherever they are and whenever they live. Theologians today use the term "anonymous Christian" to identify persons living the life of grace without knowing Christ specifically. They are being saved by the same divine power at work among visible Church members.

Should this doctrine of anonymous Christianity put a damper on the Church's missionary impetus? If pagans can be saved whether they hear the gospel or not, what is the need of sending missionaries to preach to them of

Jesus Christ and salvation through faith and baptism? To be consistent, wouldn't the Council Fathers have to mute the old teaching about the missionary apostolate of the Church? But the Council did no such thing. It emphasized the missionary role of the Church more than ever. "The pilgrim Church is missionary by her very nature" (*Ad Gentes*, no. 2). The Council made it clear that it was speaking of missionary activity in the strict sense; it did not mean to say that the Church is missionary because all her work is, in a certain way, the evangelization of pagans.

The ultimate reason for the missionary task of the Church is the will of God that all men be saved and come to the knowledge of truth. Jesus came as the Savior of all men, and his mandate to the Church is a command of universal proclamation of the gospel:

> Full authority has been given to me both in heaven and on earth; go, therefore, and make disciples of all the nations. Baptize them in the name of the Father, and of the Son, and of the Holy Spirit (Mt 28:18-19).

The Council sees missionary activity as an expression of the love of Christians welling forth into the world:

> The members of the Church are impelled to carry on such missionary activity by reason of the love with which they love God and by which they desire to share with all men in the spiritual goods of both this life and the life to come (*Ad Gentes*, no. 7).

Old Testament

A brief review of the Israelite attitude toward missionary activity will serve as a helpful backdrop for New Testament teaching and Church interpretation. The proclamation of universal salvation comes early in the Bible, in the Yahwist author's story of the call of Abraham.

> I will make of you a great nation,
>   and I will bless you;
> I will make your name great,
>   so that you will be a blessing.
> I will bless those who bless you
>   and curse those who curse you.
> All the communities of the earth
>   shall find blessing in you (Gn 12:2-3).

This passage follows the story of the Tower of Babel. The division and dispersal of peoples will be overcome in a salvation that will be for all.

Though this idea of universal salvation is present in the Israelite Scriptures, it was not a controlling vision for most of Israel's history. The Hebrews had to carve out a place for themselves from among pagans who worshiped other gods. They exterminated as much of this foreign cult as they could, and were constantly on guard against its influence in Israelite worship. Israel's historical writers, especially the authors of Judges and the Books of Kings, showed the successes and reversals of the nation as dependent on the people's fidelity to Yahweh or their following of other gods. This protectiveness of Yahweh's role and the purity of the cult meant hostility toward other peoples. Pagans were associated with ungodliness; they were enemies of God. It was hard to believe that Yahweh could love all without exception and desire the salvation of all.

The theme of universality was there, however, and gradually it took the form of a vision of all the nations coming in procession to Jerusalem.

> In days to come the mount of the Lord's house
> Shall be established higher than the mountains;
>   it shall rise high above the hills,

And people shall stream to it:
Many nations shall come, and say,
"Come, let us climb the mount of the Lord.
    to the house of the God of Jacob,
That he may instruct us in his ways,
    that we may walk in his paths"
                    (Mi 4:1-2; Is 2:2-3).

The concept here is not mission in the sense of going out to the nations to proclaim salvation to them. It is an attitude of waiting for the Lord to call the pagans to Jerusalem and being open to their approach.

The Israelites did not begin as monotheists. They accepted the possibility of gods of other nations, but believed that Yahweh was the God above all others, the Lord of all. Sometimes the expectation of a procession of the nations to Jerusalem is based expressly on this superiority of Yahweh:

There is none like you among the gods, O Lord,
    and there are no works like yours.
All the nations you have made shall come and worship you, O Lord,
    and glorify your name.
For you are great, and you do wondrous deeds;
    you alone are God (Ps 86:8-10).

When the People of God bore witness to the other nations, it was on home territory. Israel was like an oasis of praise to the true God in the midst of a desert of false worship:

I will give thanks to you among the peoples, O Lord.
I will chant your praise among the nations
                    (Ps 57:10).

The doctrine of universal salvation through Israel received a strong boost in the writings of the prophet of the Exile we know as Second Isaiah. Israel is called

> a light for the nations,
> To open the eyes of the blind,
>> to bring out prisoners from confinement,
>> and from the dungeon, those who live in darkness
>>> (Is 42:6-7).

These terms were later taken up by the evangelists to describe the mission of Jesus (Mt 11:4-6; Lk 1:78-79). In these late chapters of Isaiah are found the first glimmerings of a missionary role for Israel:

> I come to gather nations of every language;
>> they shall come and see my glory.
> I will set a sign among them;
>> from them I will send fugitives to the nations:
>>> to Tarshish, Put and Lud, Mosoch, Tubal and Javan,
>>> to the distant coastlands that have never heard of my fame, or seen my glory;
>>> and they shall proclaim my glory among the nations (Is 66:18-19).

Even here, though, it is not the Hebrews themselves who will carry the message. Israel will be a training center but the missionaries will come "from them."

New Testament

We search the gospels in vain for a universal ministry of Jesus beyond Israel. There are brief forays into pagan territories. Jesus went briefly into the "Gerasene territory" (Mk 5:1-20); he healed the daughter of a Syro-Phoenician woman in the area of Tyre and Sidon (Mk 7:24-30). In the latter instance, Jesus pointed out that this ministry was an exception: "It is not right to take the food of the children and throw it to the dogs."

Jesus saw his mission as first of all to the chosen People of God. He even prescribed boundaries for the first preaching mission of the Twelve: "Do not visit pagan territory and do not enter a Samaritan town. Go instead after the lost sheep of the house of Israel" (Mt 10:5-6). We know that besides occasionally responding to pleas for help outside Israel, Jesus broke conventional boundaries within Israel. He went into Samaria and talked with Samaritans. He ate with people who were considered sinners and criminals.

Jesus' teaching shows that he intended his followers to take the message of salvation beyond the confines of Israel. When he healed the servant of the centurion, an outsider within Israel, he took the occasion to pay tribute to a Gentile's faith and to warn the Jews about their complacency: "Many will come from the east and the west and will find a place at the banquet in the kingdom of God with Abraham, Isaac, and Jacob, while the natural heirs of the kingdom will be driven out into the dark" (Mt 8: 11-12). On another occasion he said it will go better on judgment day with Tyre and Sidon than with Chorazin and Bethsaida (Mt 11:21-22). The same sort of promise and warning are at work in the parable of the banquet (Lk 14:16-24; Mt 22:2-10). The people who were first invited to the banquet have refused to come. Their place will be taken by others. Jesus leaves it to the imagination of his listeners to identify the characters in the story. He even says that the Jews of his generation will be judged by the inhabitants of Nineveh and the queen of the South (Mt 12:41-42). The universal mission Jesus foresaw would have to await the victory of his death-resurrection and the outpouring of the Holy Spirit.

The post-resurrection community soon saw the clear lines of a universal missionary mandate in these words and actions of Jesus. The infancy stories of Matthew and Luke illustrate this faith of the Church of their own time. In Matthew's account magi from the East, pagans, bring gifts to Jesus, symbolically paying the homage of their own nations to the one who will be revealed as their savior. In the Gospel of Luke, Simeon proclaims Jesus the minister of universal salvation:

> Now, Master, you can dismiss your servant in peace;
>   you have fulfilled your word.
> For my eyes have witnessed your saving deed
>   displayed for all the peoples to see:
> A revealing light to the Gentiles,
>   the glory of your people Israel (2:29-32).

Acts of the Apostles

The proclamation of the gospel and bearing witness to all nations is the special mandate of the Church in the Acts of the Apostles. In his Gospel, Luke traced Jesus' journey from Galilee to Jerusalem; in Acts the Church takes Jesus' message of salvation from Jerusalem to Rome, which represents "the ends of the earth" (1:8). The Holy Spirit won by Jesus in his death and resurrection is the universal gift of salvation. The Spirit is also the guide of the apostolic mission as it makes its way across the Mediterranean lands. Peter and John tell their accusers that they cannot be silent about Jesus; they must tell what they have seen and heard (4:20). Peter indicates the universal sweep of Jesus' victory in quoting the promise to Abraham in his speech to the crowd at the Temple: "In your offspring, all the families of the earth shall be blessed" (3:25).

It is revealed at Paul's conversion that he is to play a special role in taking the gospel beyond Israel. "This man is the instrument I have chosen to bring my name to the Gentiles" (9:15). He is part of the community at

Antioch that begins to proclaim Christ among the Greeks. Soon the parent community in Jerusalem must examine the case to see if it is really God's will that non-Jews be accepted in the Church. Barnabas is sent first and is convinced that this is a genuine development: "He rejoiced to see the evidence of God's favor" (11:23). Later Paul and Barnabas come to Jerusalem to explain their mission. It is authenticated for the whole Church (15:1-29). Missionary bands are then sent into the Gentile territories to call all people to salvation in Jesus Christ.

In his own writings, Paul reveals how strongly he felt his missionary mandate. He was not to settle down and build up communities but to light fires of faith by spreading the word of God: "Christ did not send me to baptize, but to preach the gospel" (1 Cor 1:17; cf. Rm 15:20-21). "Preaching the gospel is not the subject of a boast; I am under compulsion and have no choice" (1 Cor 9:16). His preaching is an act of love. He is sharing with the Gentiles the life he has been given. It is an act of generation. "You have ten thousand guardians in Christ but you have only one father. It was I who begot you in Christ Jesus through the preaching of the gospel" (1 Cor 4:15). Paul understood his missionary vocation as a "priestly duty" which led him to "fulfill the gospel" by proclaiming it in as wide an area as possible (Rm 15: 15-21).

The Acts of the Apostles presents Christian mission in terms of Luke's rich theology of the word of God. Conversion is "accepting the word" (Ac 2:41; 8:14). A principal effect of the coming of the Holy Spirit is the ability to speak the word of God "with boldness" (4:31). The word is not only a message but the agent of community formation. By its power, diverse elements are molded into a Church. Listening to the word is one of the characteristic practices of the new community (2:42). Growth in membership in the community is ex-

pressed by the awkward expression "The word of God
grew" (6:7; 12:24; 19:20). The gospel preachers are
described as "ministers of the word" (6:4; cf. Lk 1:2).
"Word" here is especially rich in ambiguity: it has blended
the meanings of message, community, and even the person of Jesus.

By this use of word terminology, Luke draws the
complete circle of involvement with the word of God.
The word is first of all a message of salvation addressed
to the listener. If a person responds in faith he is drawn
into the community of believers. Sharing life with other
believers is an essential consequence of accepting the word
and believing in Jesus. As the community preaches the
word, its very life becomes part of the proclamation.
The faithful hearer of the word becomes the word of God
to others. Pope John XXIII described this same reality
when he spoke of the Christian as the "eighth sacrament,
the only one many people will ever receive."

The Church's Missionary Role

Our brief review of the biblical material gives warrant
to Vatican II's declaration that the Church is "missionary
by her very nature" (*Ad Gentes,* no. 2). But it remains
to be seen how this is so today, given the "problem" of the
universality of saving grace mentioned at the beginning
of this chapter. If grace is available without the preaching
of the gospel, what does the missionary vocation of the
Church amount to?

The missionary task of the Church means that she is
"divinely sent to all nations that she might be the universal sacrament of salvation" (*Ad Gentes,* no. 1). Though
redemptive grace is universally present, the Church is
raised up among the nations to identify this saving power
as the power of Christ and to open up to men the true
meaning of their existence. It is in this way that St. Paul
praised the Athenians for worshiping an Unknown God,

but made explicit in terms of Christ what they were groping for uncertainly: "What you are thus worshiping in ignorance I intend to make known to you" (Ac 17:23).

The Church does not exist as a refuge for her children, but as sign and instrument of salvation for the world. The Council was careful to emphasize this outward thrust of the missionary apostolate. It has often been said that every work of the Church is missionary in a certain sense. But this can be an escape, a word game. If everything is missionary work, nothing is. The Decree on the Church's Missionary Activity makes a careful distinction between "pastoral" activity where the Church is already visible and "missionary" activity where the Church is not yet implanted (no. 8). Work in ghettos and rural areas in America may be missionary in a broad sense, but it is pastoral in the sense of Vatican II. The Council did not back down here. It noted rather that the Church's primary commitment is missionary in this strict sense, while the pastoral task of serving the already established Church, while important, is secondary in order of priority. If the missionary task is not being done, every other work of the Church, no matter how excellent, is somehow called into question.

In proclaiming the message to mission territories the Church does not "bring salvation" in from the outside, but helps the anonymous grace present germinate into living and visible Christian faith. The grace of Christ is incarnatory; that is, it aims toward taking flesh and becoming visible to the world. Missionaries see the truth and grace among the nations as "a sort of secret presence of God" and work to "lay bare the seeds of the word which lie hidden there" (*Ad Gentes*, nos. 9, 11).

A Missionary Attitude

Christ is the Light who "gives light to every man" (Jn 1:9). The presupposition of the missionary must be that the grace of Christ has already reached the unevan-gelized in God's own mysterious way (*Gaudium et Spes*, no. 22). The missionary's responsibility is to confirm faith, grace, and truth; and to do this effectively he must form the attitude of expecting these divine realities to be present already at least germinally. The Christian mis-sionary, and in an important sense that means every be-liever, must give the benefit of the doubt to grace. An initial reflex suspicion of persons is a sign of some unre-deemed sinfulness in a Christian. It is a lack of faith in the power of God to reach all men with the power of salvation.

Instead of being suspicious and hostile, we must learn to expect good in people of other religious traditions and in people with no clear religious orientation. There is no place for a feeling of superiority over the religions and cultures that produced in our time men like Gandhi, Camus, Schweitzer and Hammarskjöld. Echoing the Fathers of the Church, the Council speaks of the goodness and truth among pagan civilizations as "a preparation for the gospel" (*Ad Gentes*, no. 3).Whatever good is found to be sown in the hearts and minds of men, or in the rites and cultures peculiar to various peoples, is not lost. One remembers the self-righteous consternation aroused when Pope John implied the possibility of good in the Marxist movement. The Council does more than admit that final salvation may be somehow attained outside the visible Church: a *life of grace* may be lived there, too.

Those who have taken to heart their vocation in a missionary Church will be hesitant to judge the merit of another person's religious observance but eager to help anyone achieve the full expression of Catholic faith. There is nothing to be gained by forcing a person to be-lieve our way; this is in fact forbidden (*Ad Gentes*, no. 13). But there is much to be gained by helping the person who is searching. A missionary attitude helps people find the true meaning of their existence in the visible Church of Christ. But our main concern as servants of the truth is that each person be honest before God in the depths of his own heart. Without this, there is no salvation inside or outside the Church; with this, a person can be saved by the grace of Christ wherever he is found.

READING SUGGESTIONS

Vatican Council II, *Decree on the Church's Missionary Activity (Ad Gentes)*.

Anderson, G. H. and Stransky, T. F. *Mission Trends No. 1: Crucial Issues in Mission Today*. New York: Paulist and Grand Rapids: Eerdmans, 1974.

Hillman, Eugene. *The Church as Mission*. New York: Herder and Herder, 1965.

Power, John. *Mission Theology Today*. Maryknoll, N. Y.: Orbis Books, 1971.